EARLY WORKS

1950s to 1980s

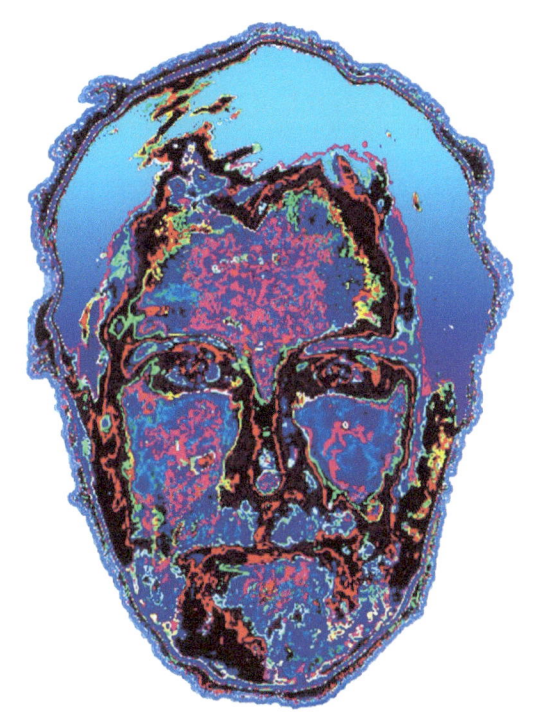

by Richard Fisher

Website: http://www.MINDWORKSart.com
Email: richardfisher@mindworksart.com

Title ID: 5137608
ISBN-13: 978-1505274936

Printed by CreateSpace.com

Front Cover: *EARLY WORKS*

The origin of this image is a
photo of my head which was
modified in the computer. It was
also used to generate the *OzHead*
(title page) using filters in
Photoshop.

Back Cover: *Four Glass Objects*

"Spirituality is my work.
The two are inseparable."
~DAVID ELLSWORTH

Introduction

One's ego-mask, the persona, was not apparent to me for many years. It is only recently that I have become more aware of it and the role it plays in our lives. It is more clear now that since the beginning of my artistic life a higher self has played an important, albeit an unconscious role...that in fact I have always been a channel for these images, these designs and artworks that have come through me. Of course it seemed that "I" did it, that I created all these images. But of course it is not true and it is liberating to know that I am "the way"...the channel of this work.

During my life I have explored many avenues of artistic possibilities; the common thread has always been visual arts...graphic and decorative design for printing on the surfaces of various products, always outward-oriented. Gradually I turned inward. There is an inward focus and an outward focus to our lives; outwardly the focus, for me, was what could be created, what would sell, be acceptable. This was my life in the industrial design world, designing and teaching in all it's aspects. Always the marketplace was kept in mind.

Inward focus became possible with fine arts, studying oil painting at the Brooklyn Museum with Reuben Tam, and later printmaking at Columbia University, Teachers' College. A wonderful tool for turning inward is the work of Betty Edwards, *Drawing on the Right Side of the Brain* and *Drawing on the Artist Within*. There are many other influences as well: Carl Jung, Leonardo daVinci, Odilon Redon and the teachings of Eckhart Tolle, *The Power of Now.* As Tolle says, "When your consciousness is directed outward, mind and world arise. When it is directed inward it realizes its own Source and returns home into the Unmanifested." To paraphrase David Ellsworth, Spirituality is our work as well as our lives. The challenge is to become more conscious.

The images in this book are earlier works as contrasted to MINDWORKS images of more recent years. Craftmanship and technique have always interested and challenged me; it is an adventure of discovery, of failures and successes, the visual world of art opening up every step of the way. What better way to discover one's self than to be an artist.

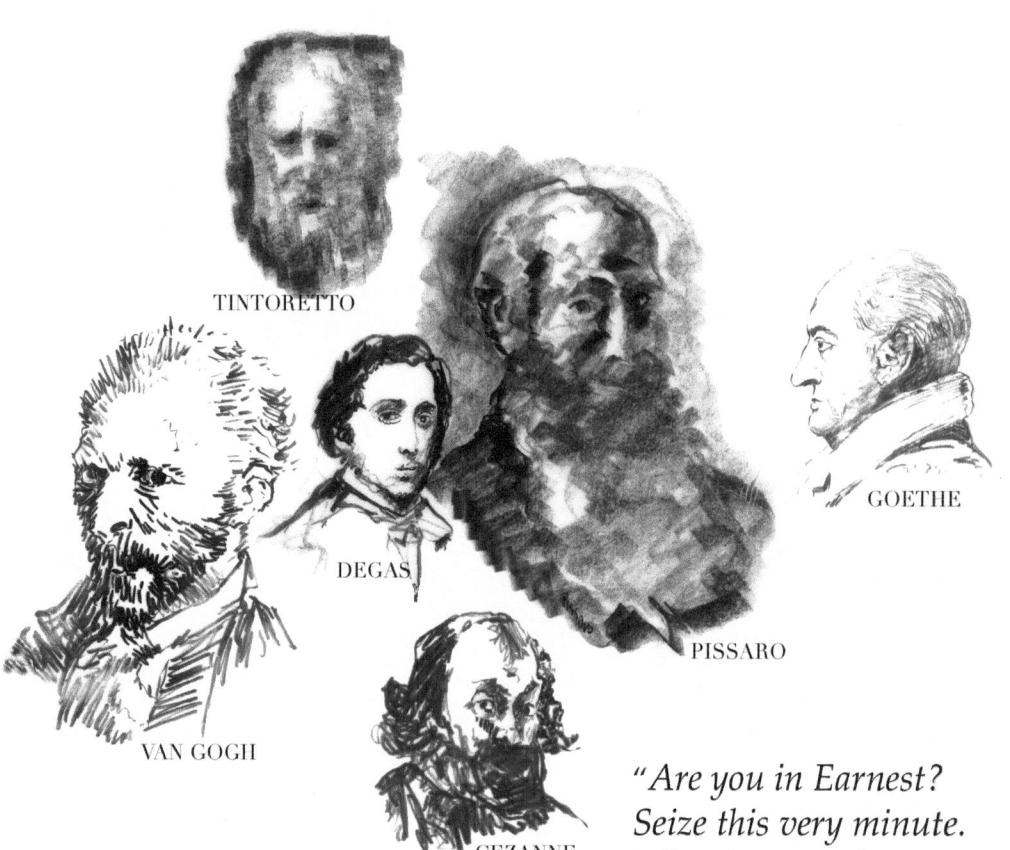

TINTORETTO

GOETHE

VAN GOGH

DEGAS

PISSARO

CEZANNE

"Are you in Earnest?
Seize this very minute.
What you can do
and Dream,
You can begin it.
Boldness has Genius,
Power and Magic in it.
Only Engage,
and the mind grows heated.
Begin...
And soon the work will be completed."

~GOETHE

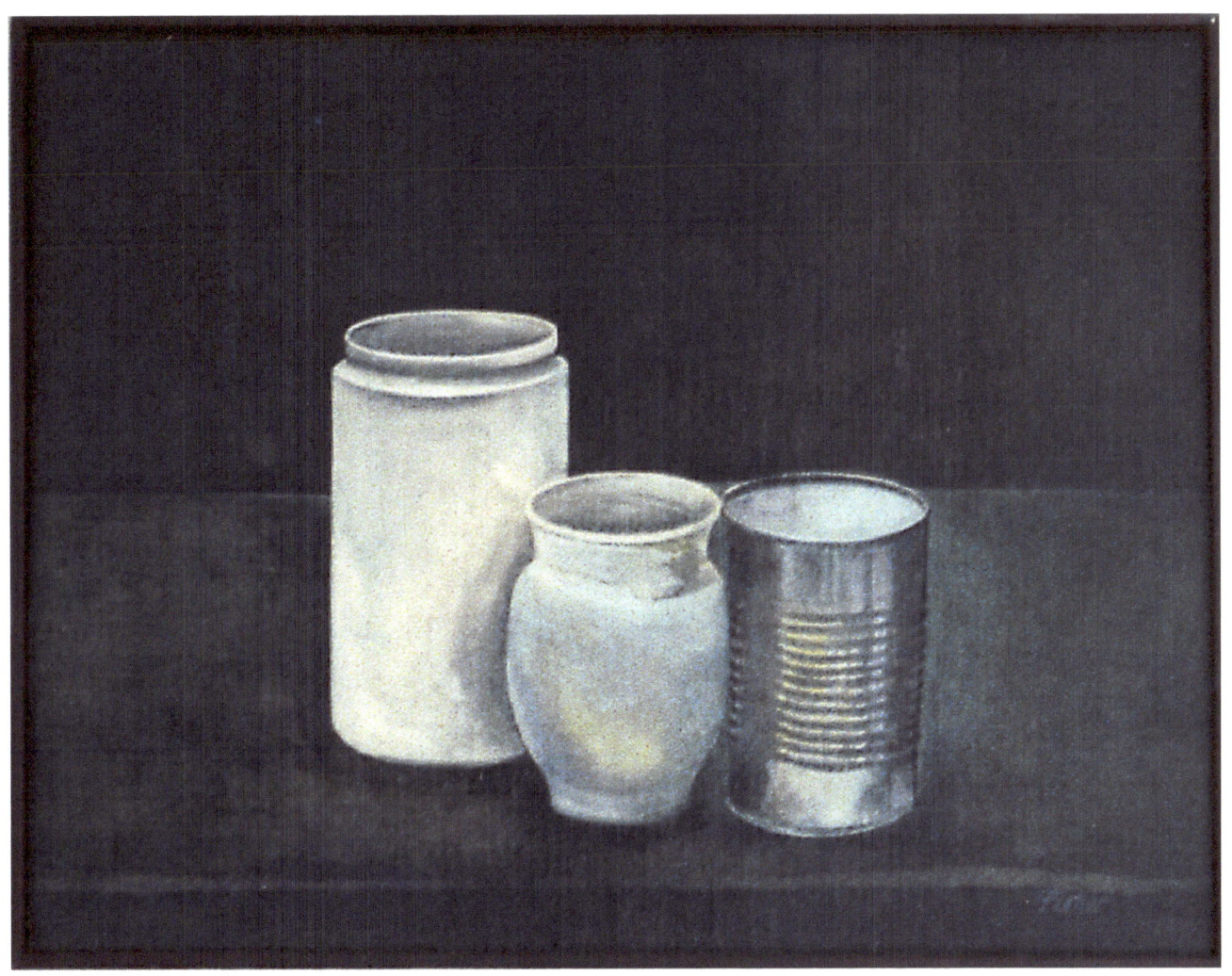

Two Clay Pots with Tin
Oil on Canvas

The first category of EARLY WORKS is
Still Life. The Oil paintings came forth
after discovering the work of Giorgio
Morandi, a metaphysical painter and
contemporary of diChirco.

1

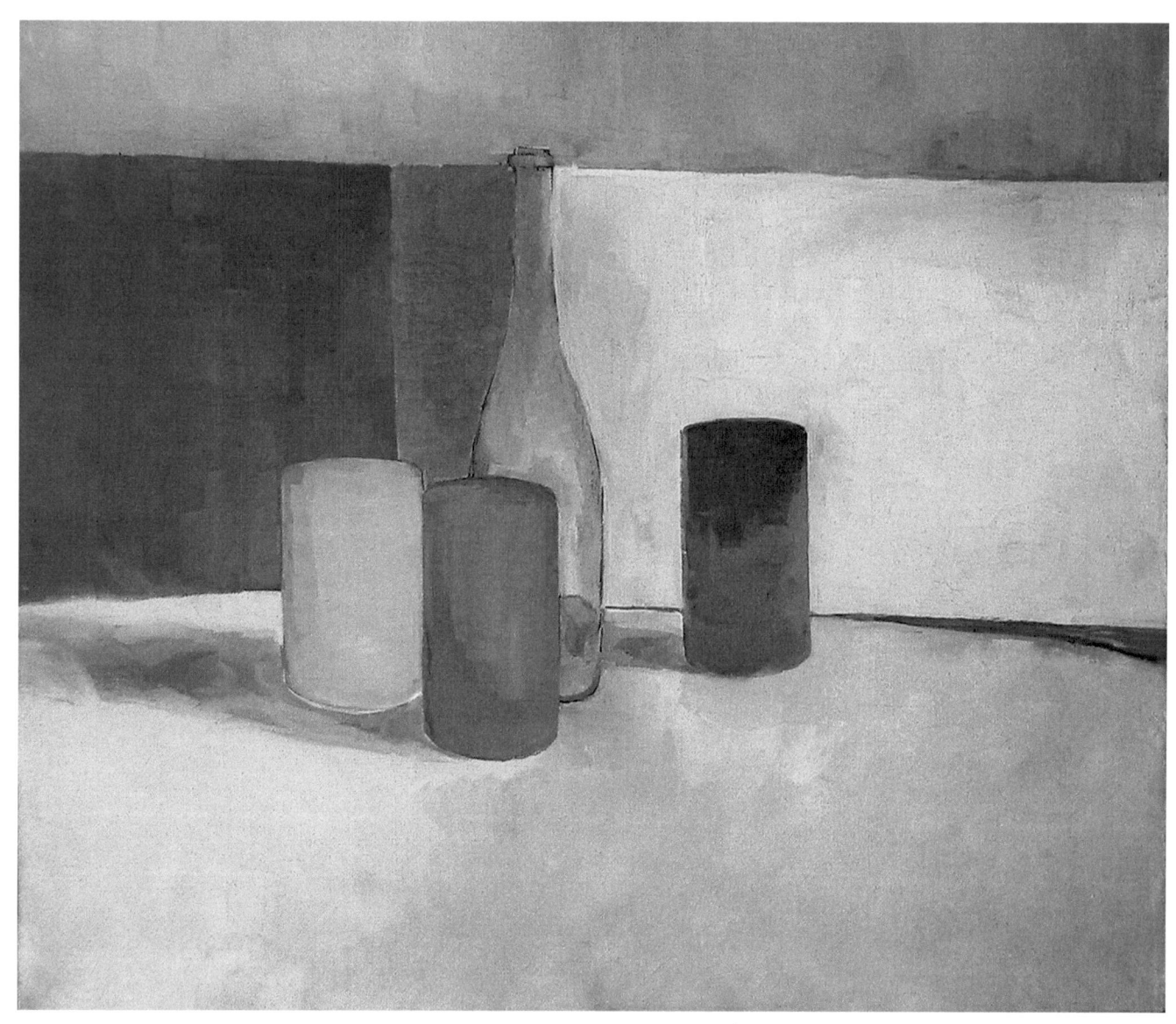

Green Still Life
Oil on Canvas

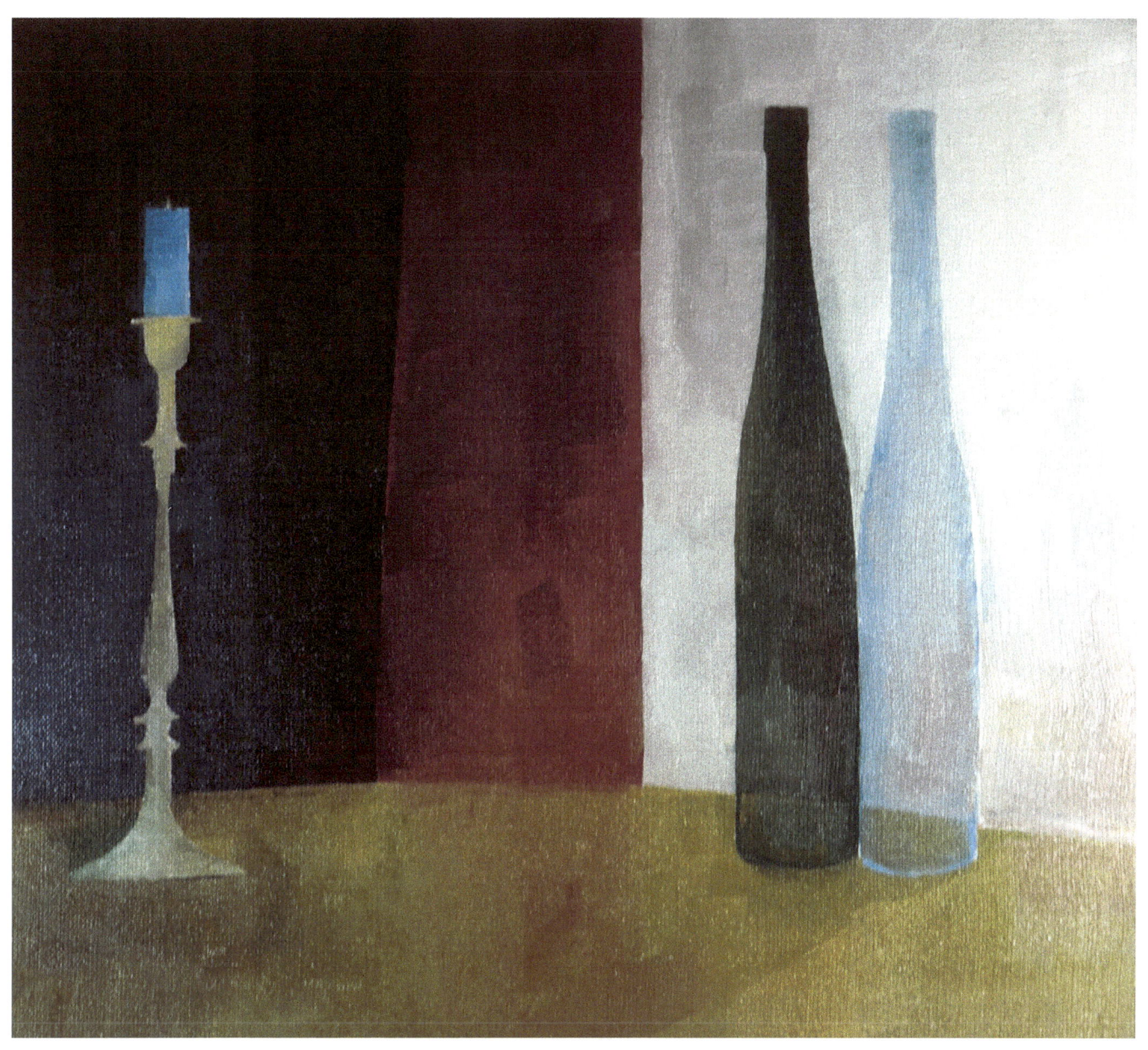

Brass Candlestick
Oil on Canvas

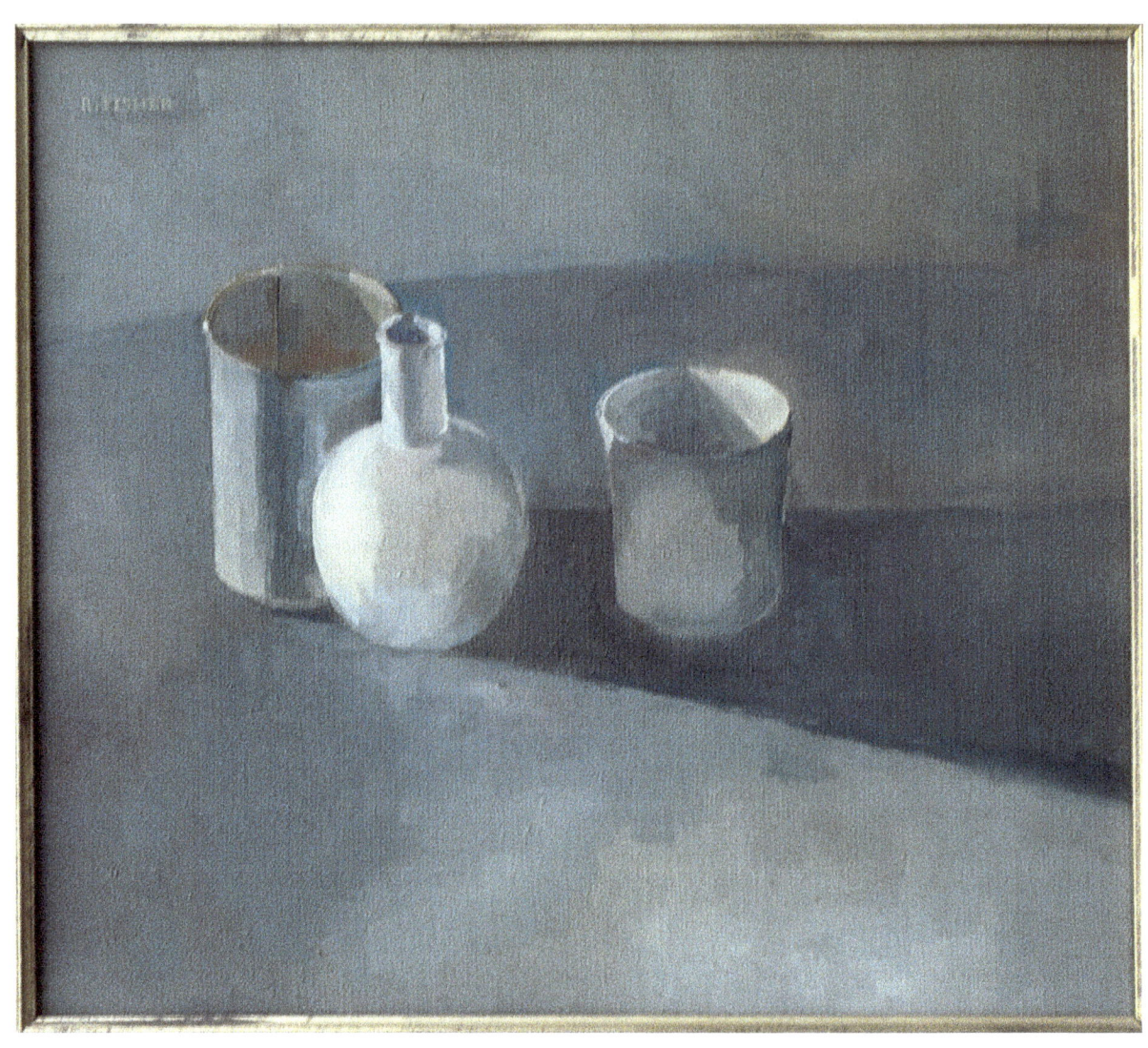

Two Small Vases and a Tin
Oil on Canvas

4

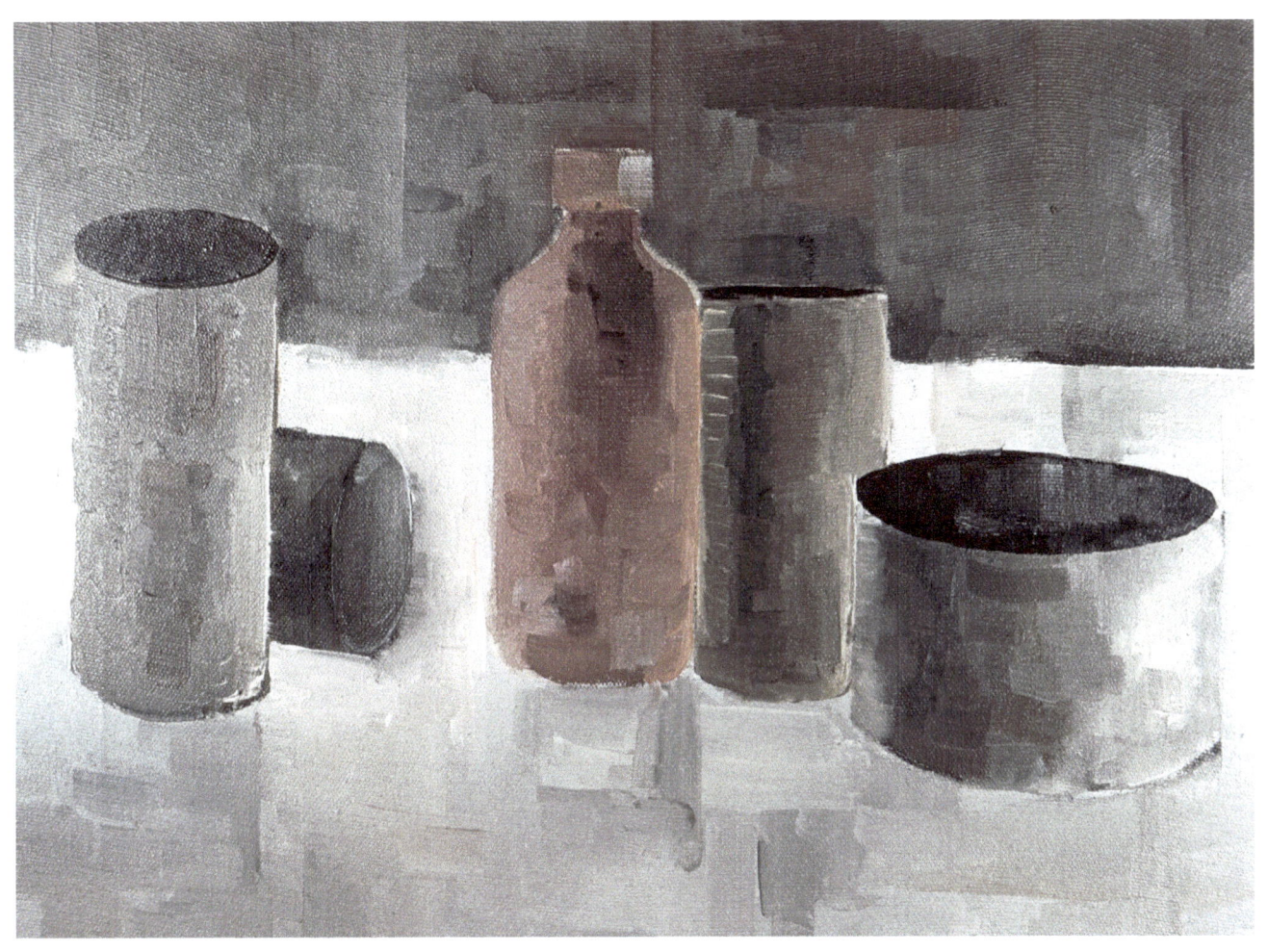

Sadness
Oil on Canvas

Reuben Tam, at the Brooklyn Museum Art School, was a very special teacher. He called this first still life "Sadness."

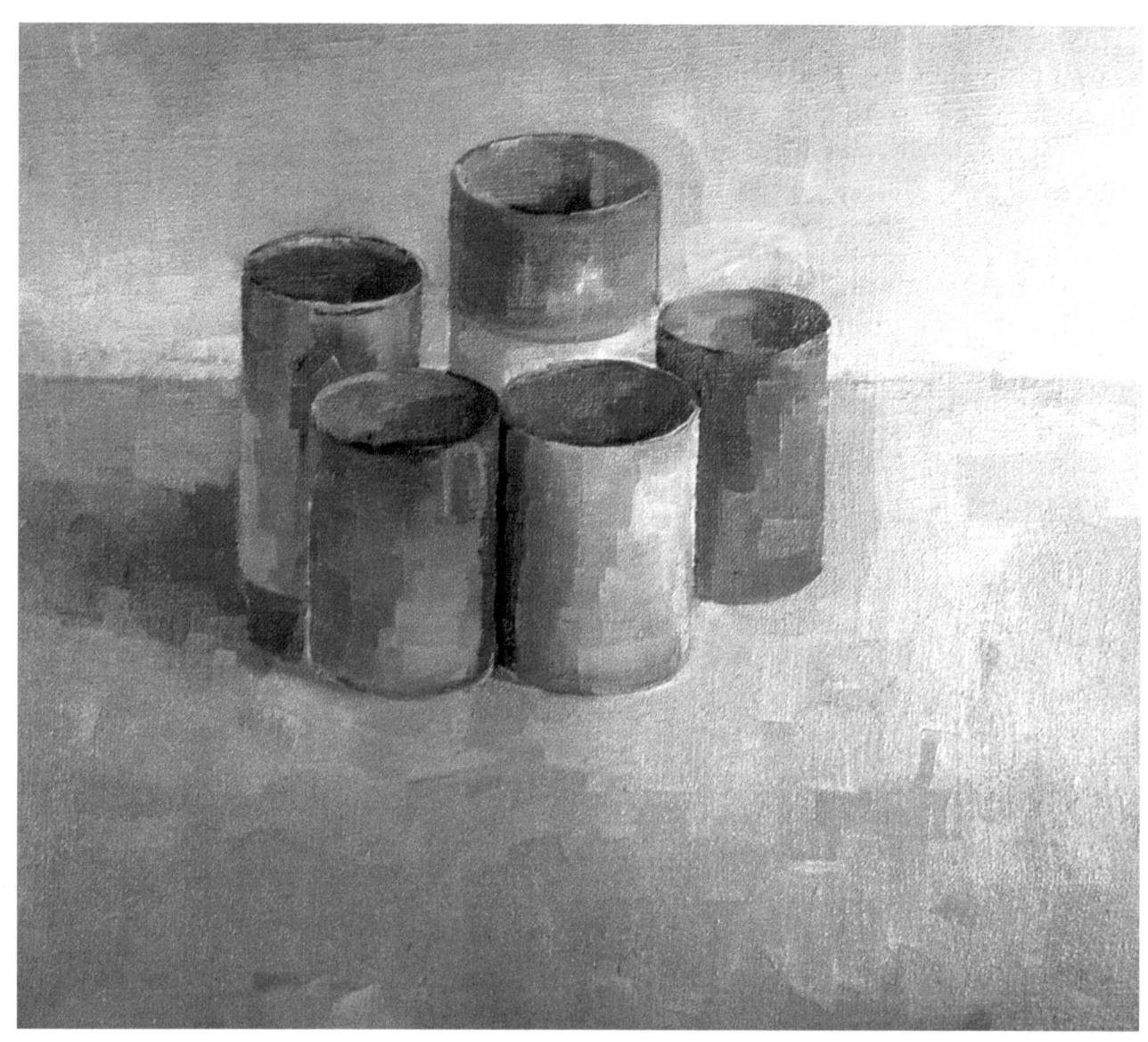

Five Tins
Oil on Canvas

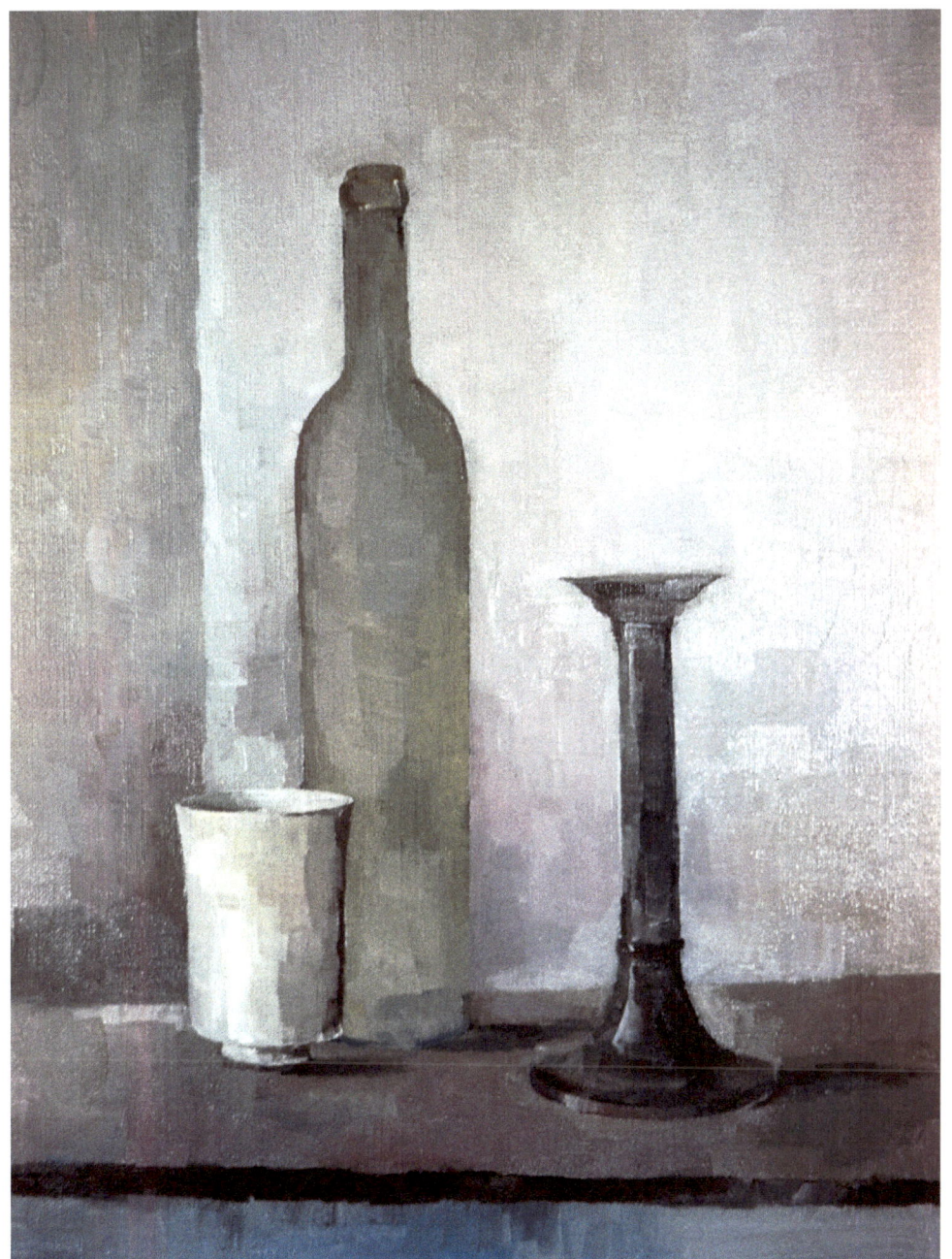

Pewter CandleStick
Oil on Canvas

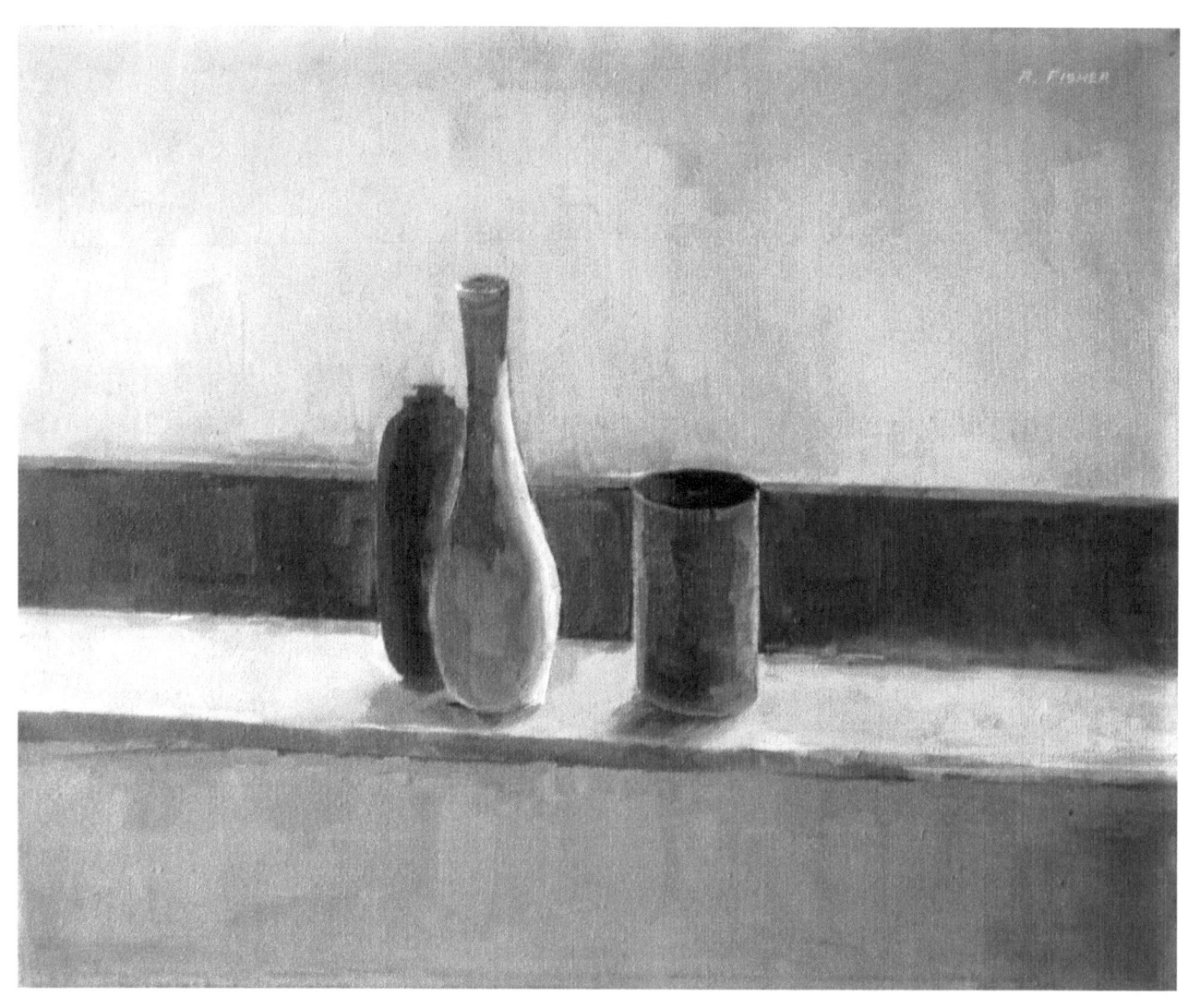

On A Windowsill
Oil on Canvas

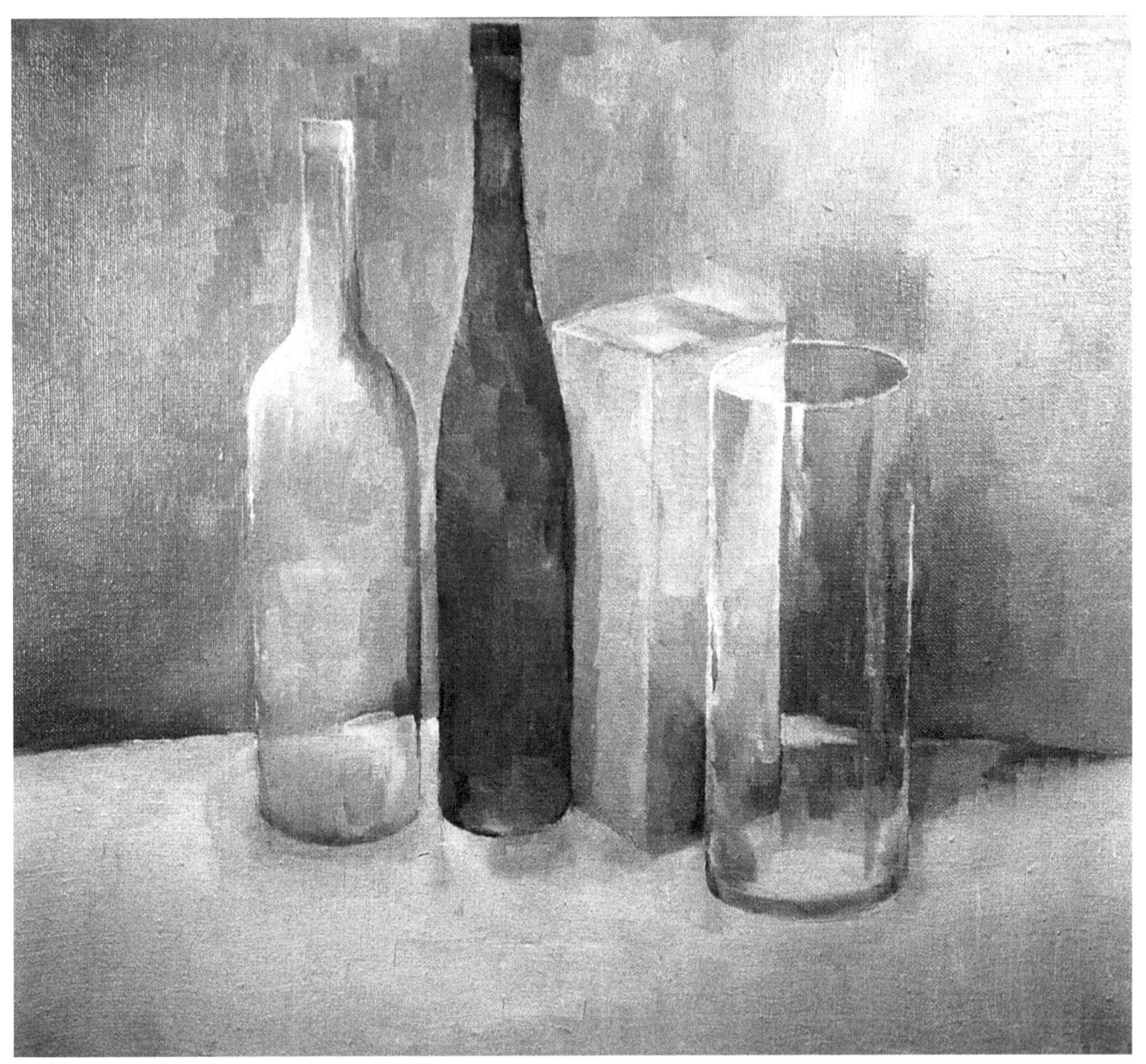

Four Tall Objects
Oil on Canvas

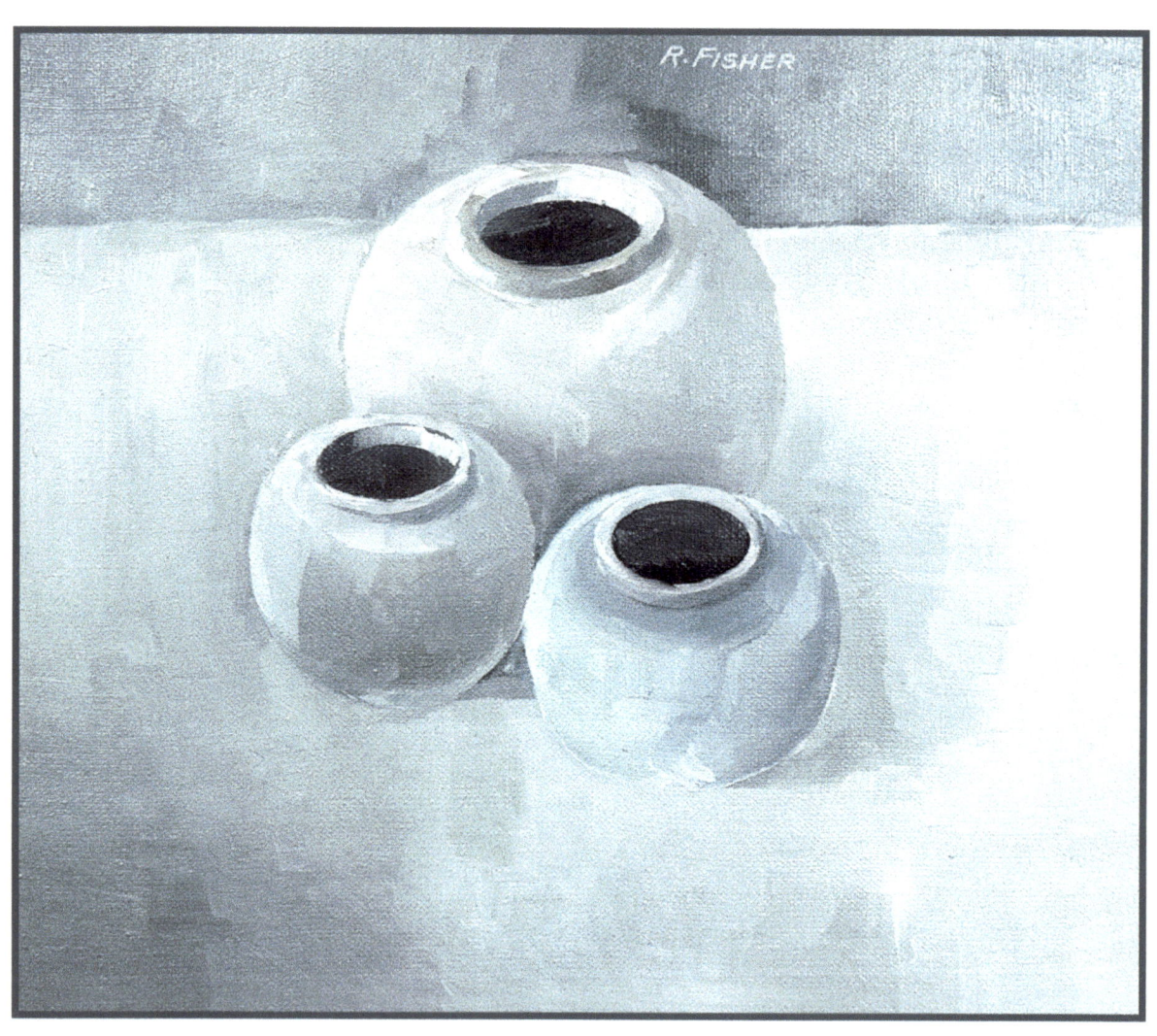

Boothbay Harbor Pots
Oil on Canvas

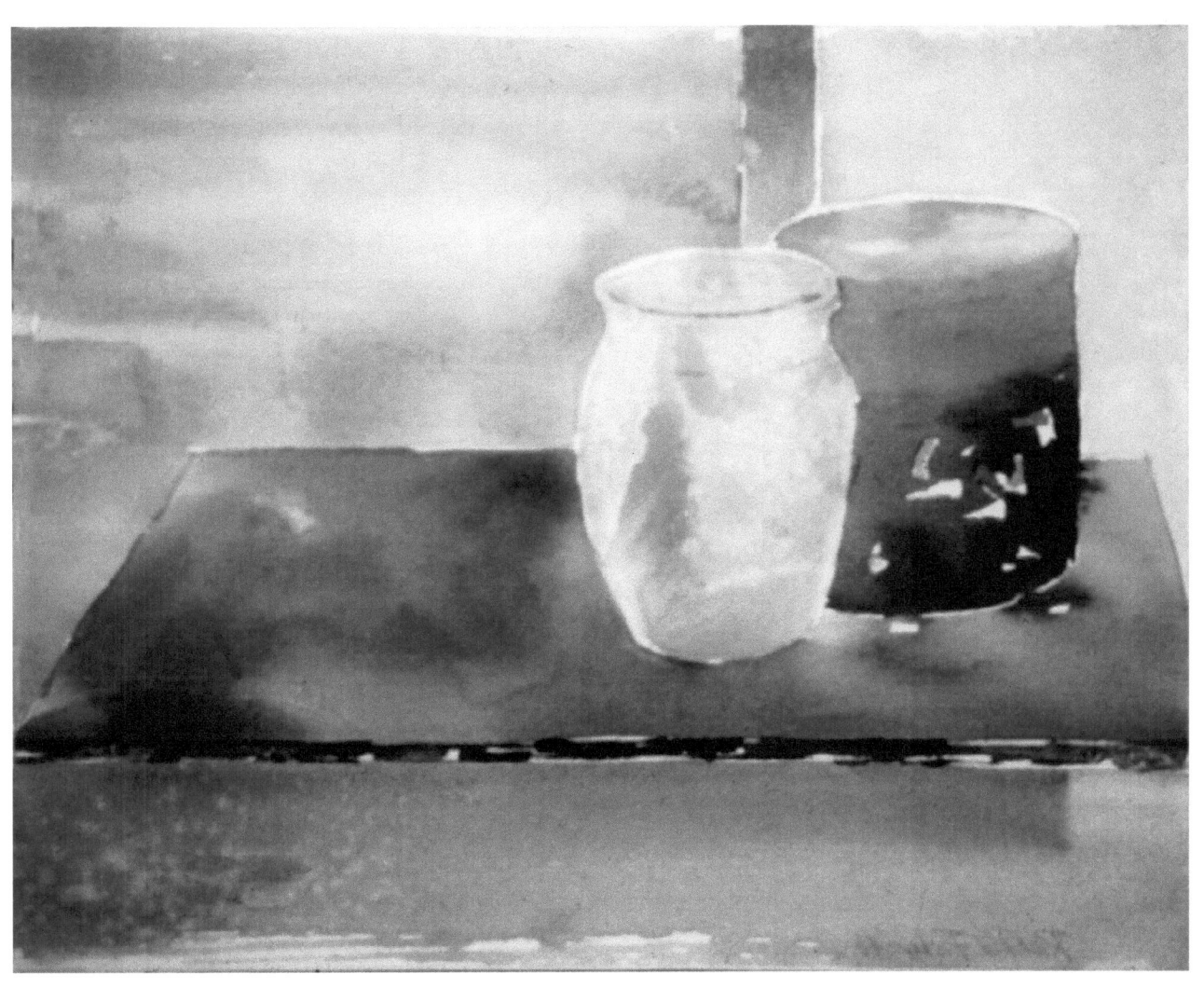

Cora's Chinese Teabox
WaterColor on paper

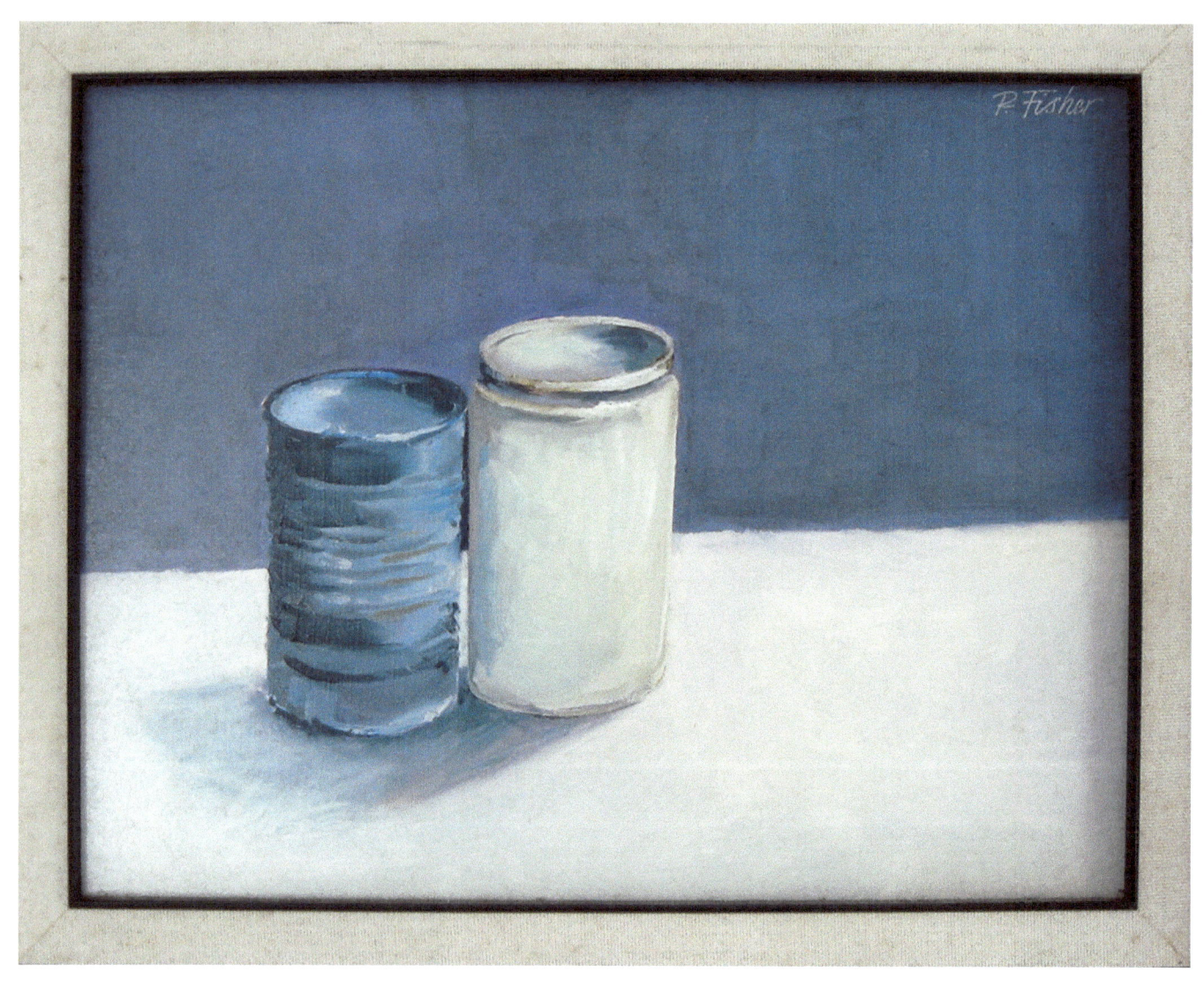

Two Containers
Oil on Canvas Board

12

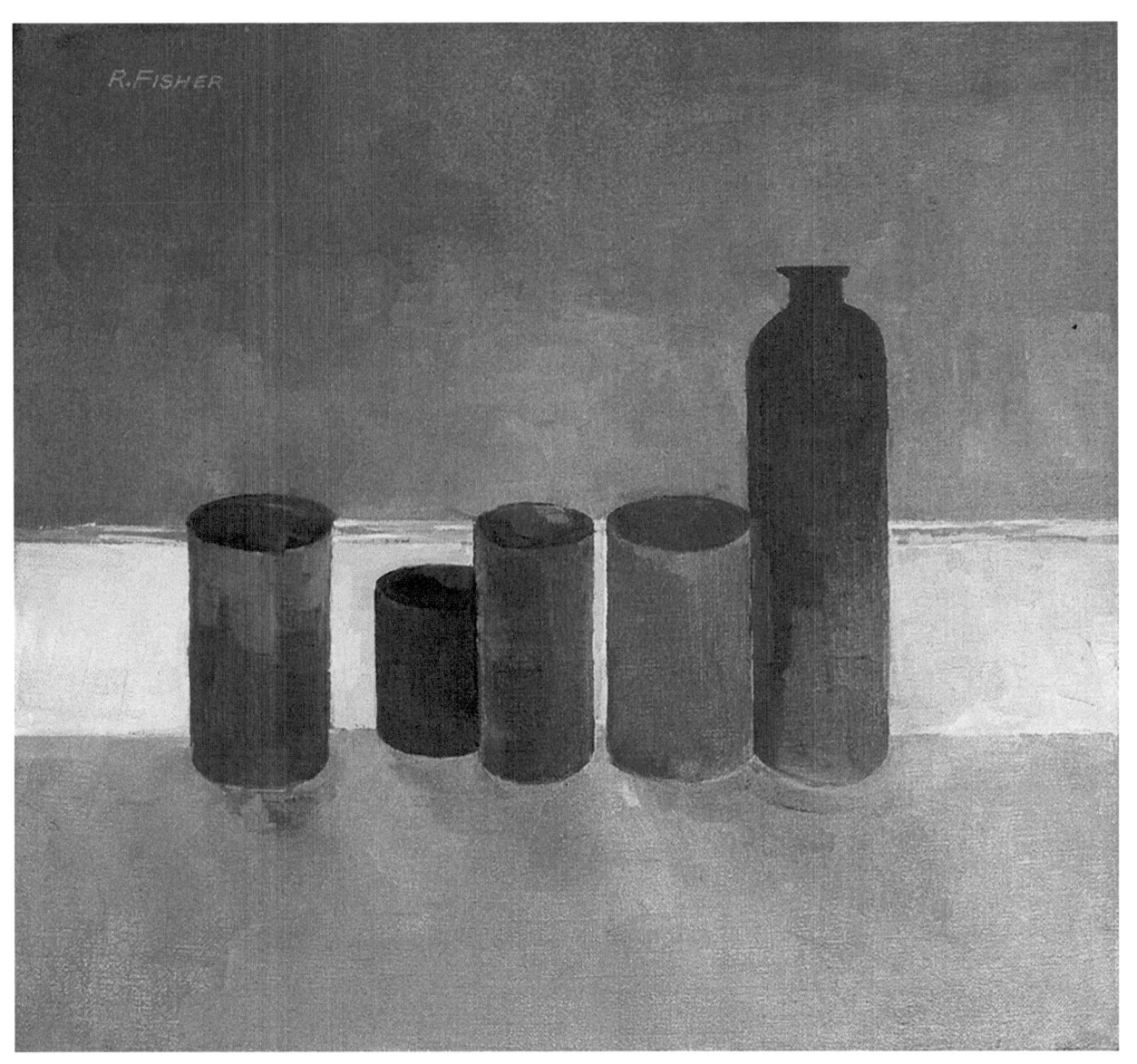

Four Tins and a Jar
Oil on Canvas

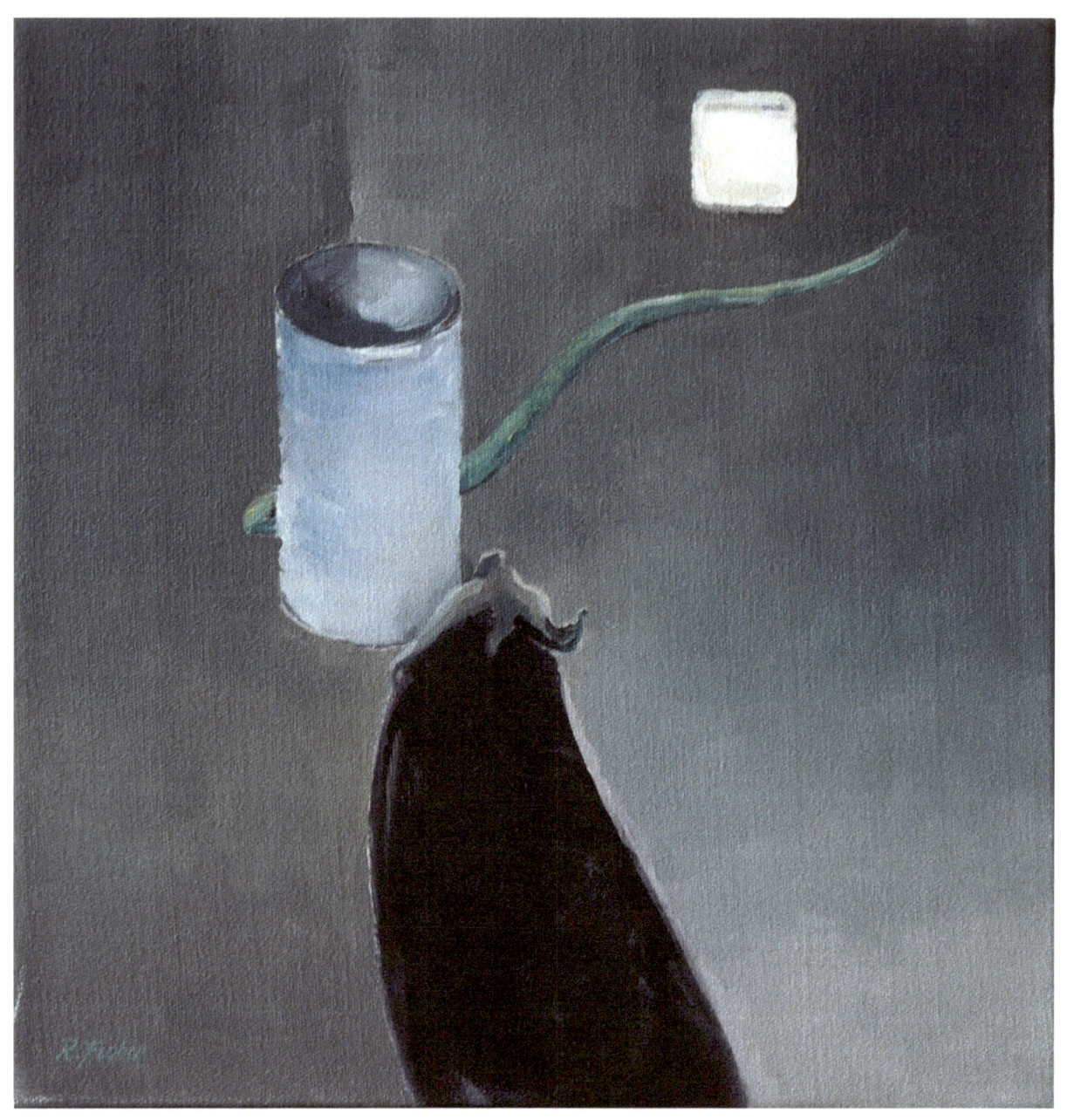

Green Snake Dream
Oil on Canvas

14

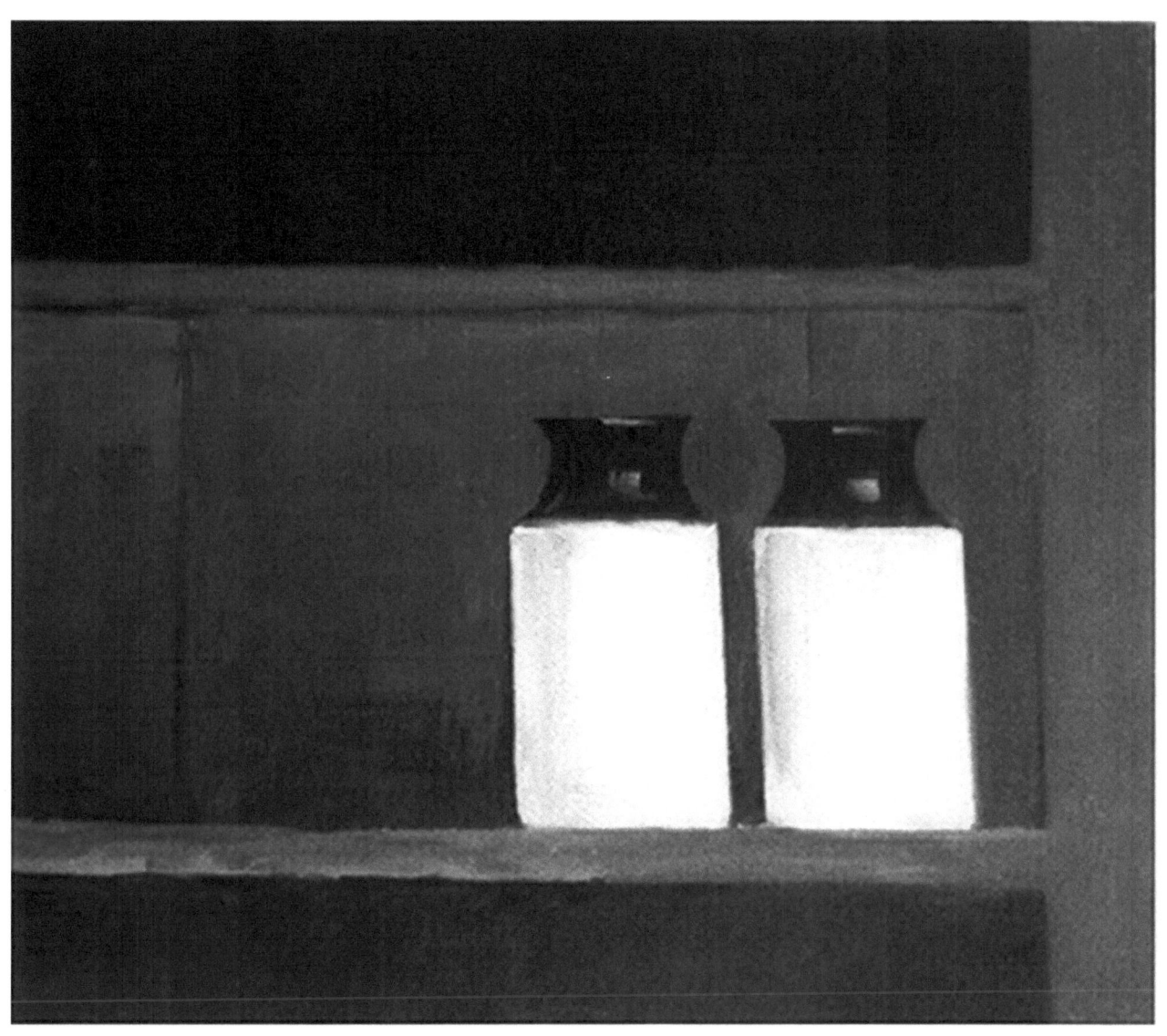

Apothecary Jars
Oil on Canvas

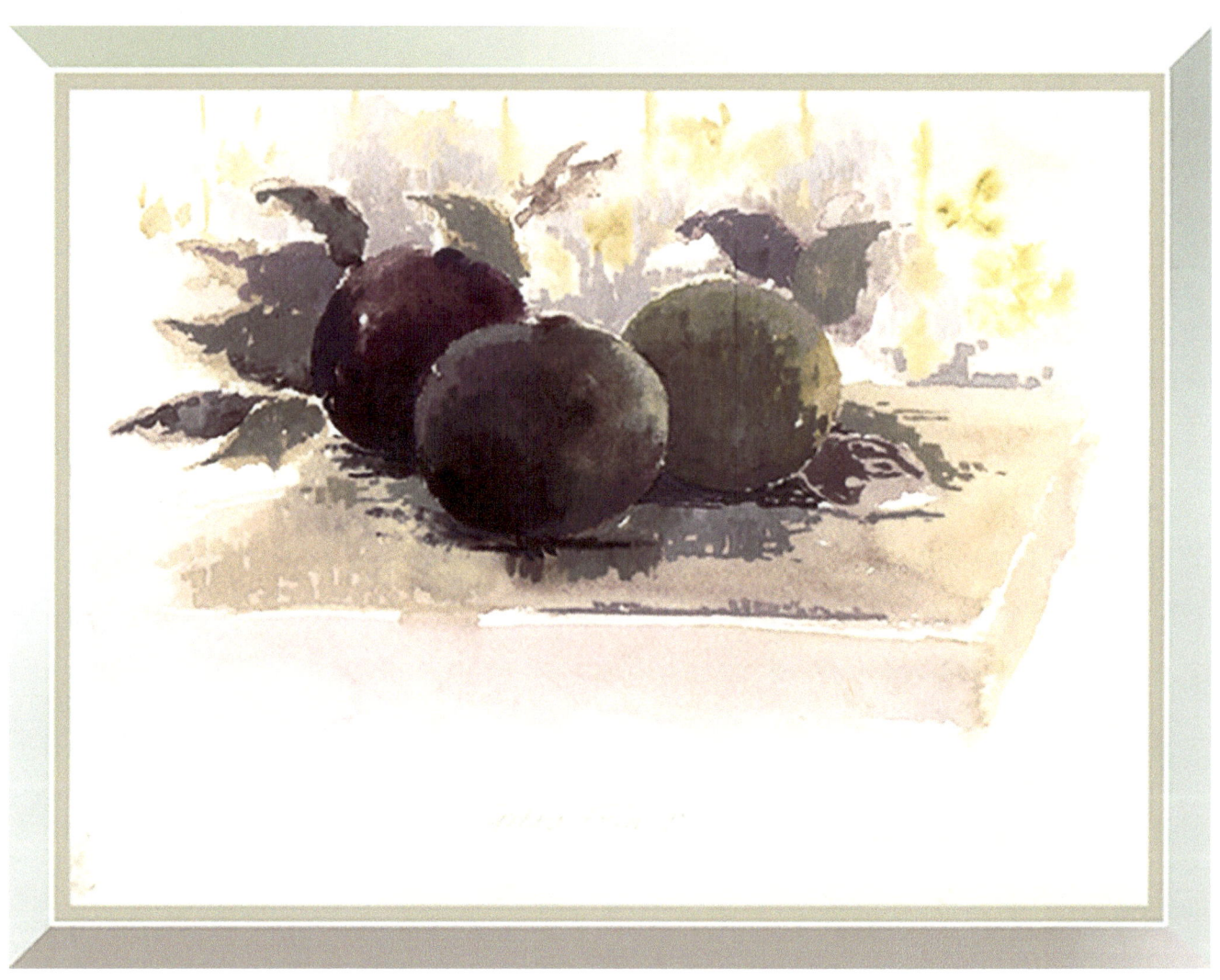

Larry's Still Life
for Isawa
Watercolor on Paper

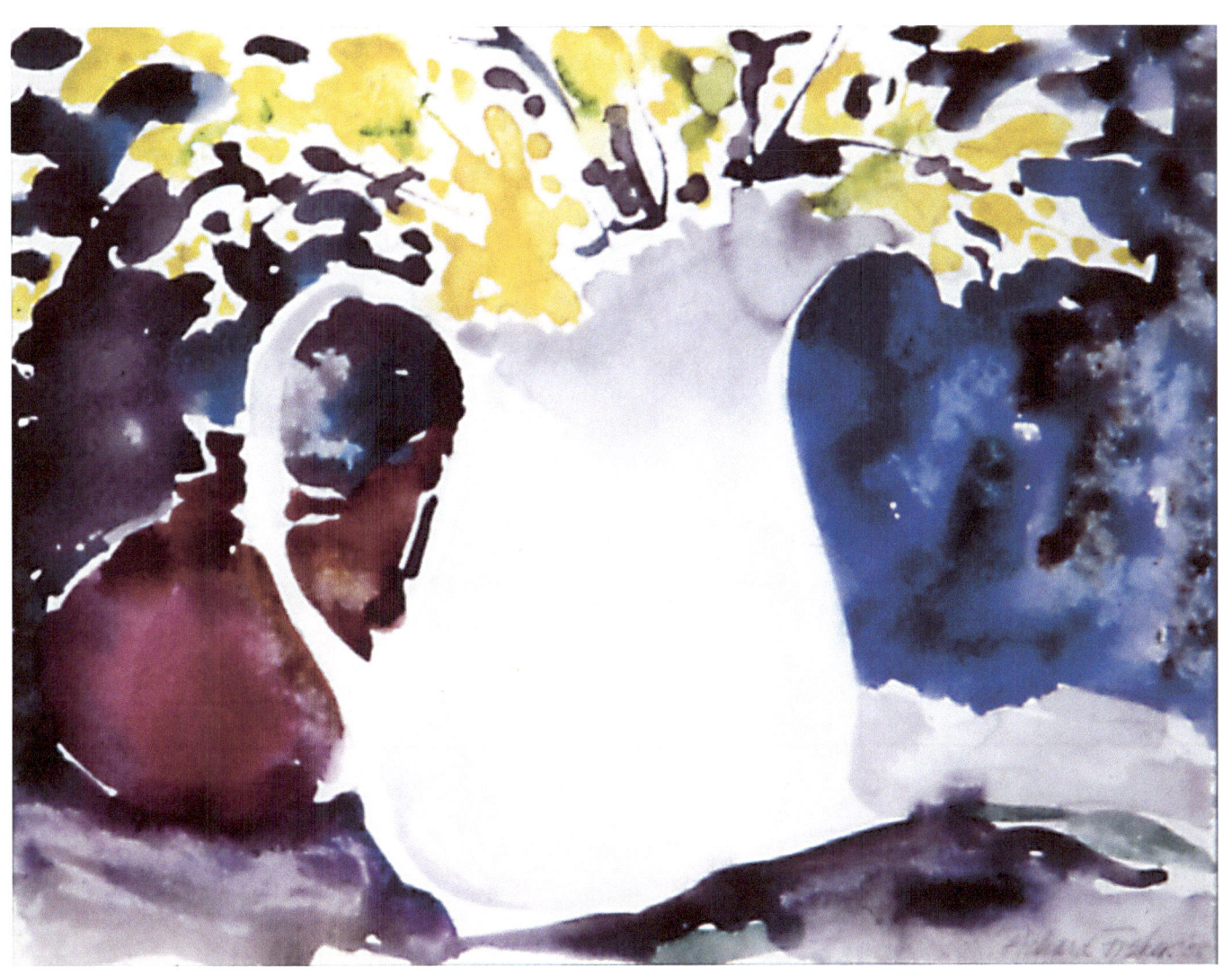

Forthysia
Watercolor on Paper

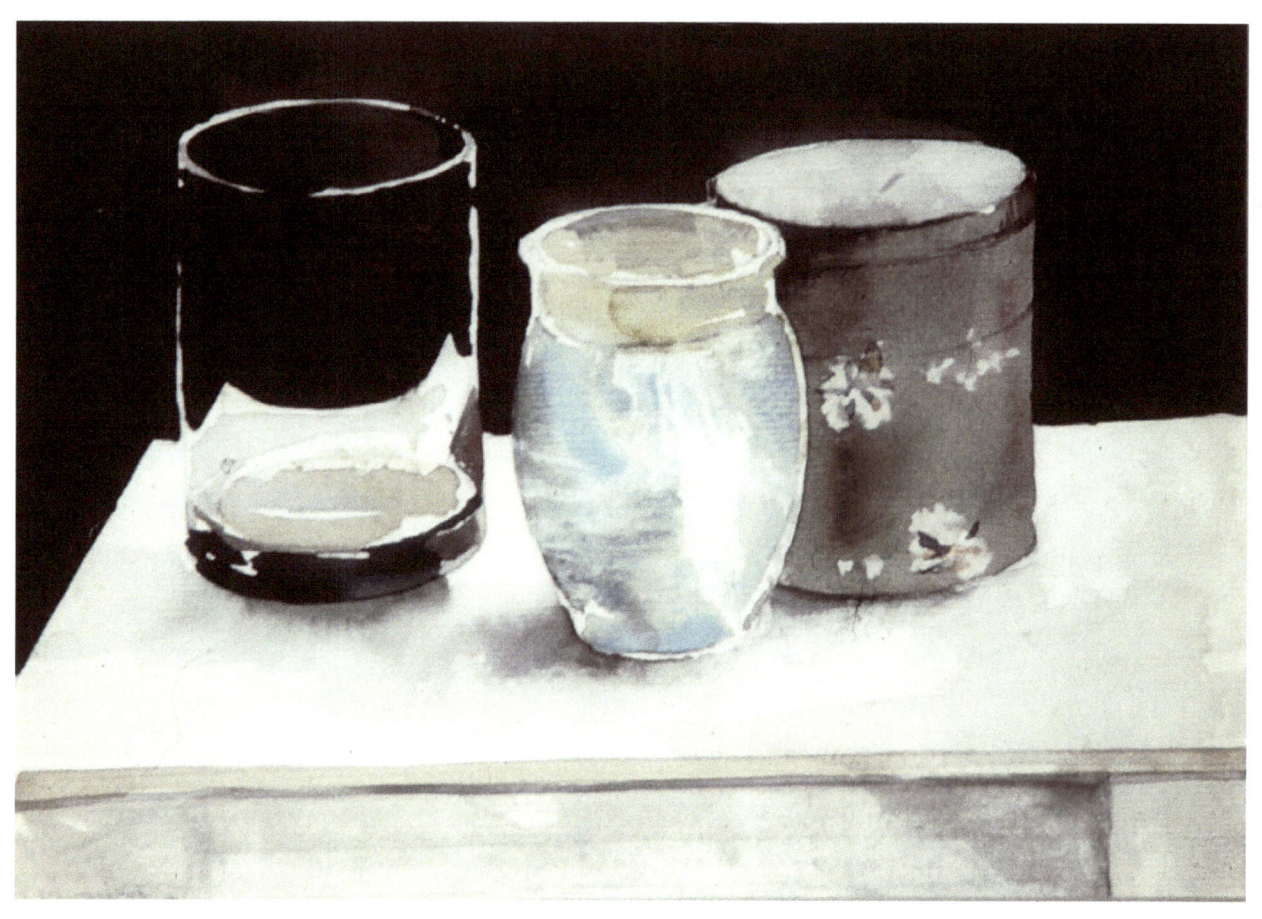

Claire's Still Life
Watercolor on Paper

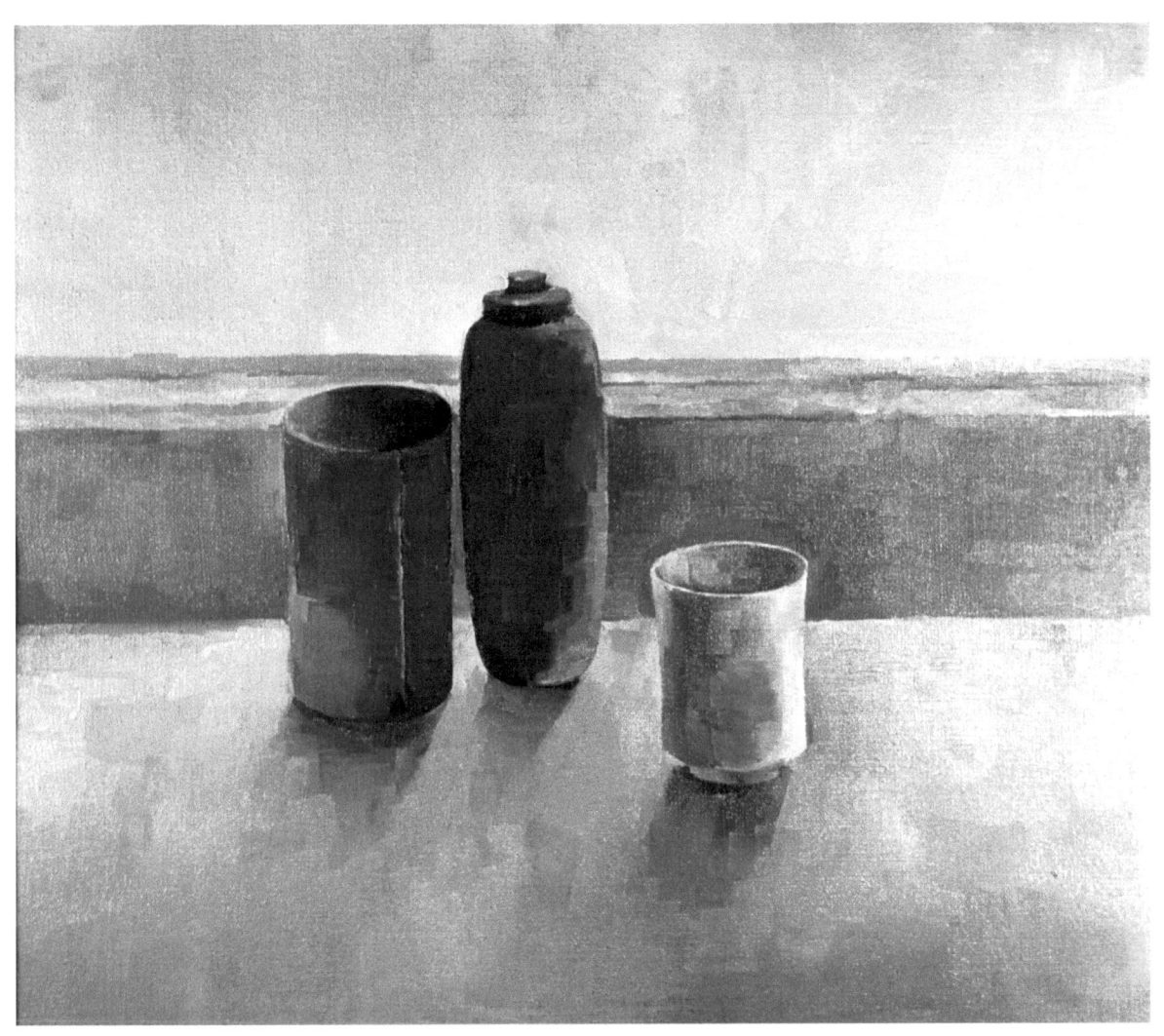

With Urn
Oil on Canvas

"Let the beauty we love
be what we do." ~Rumi

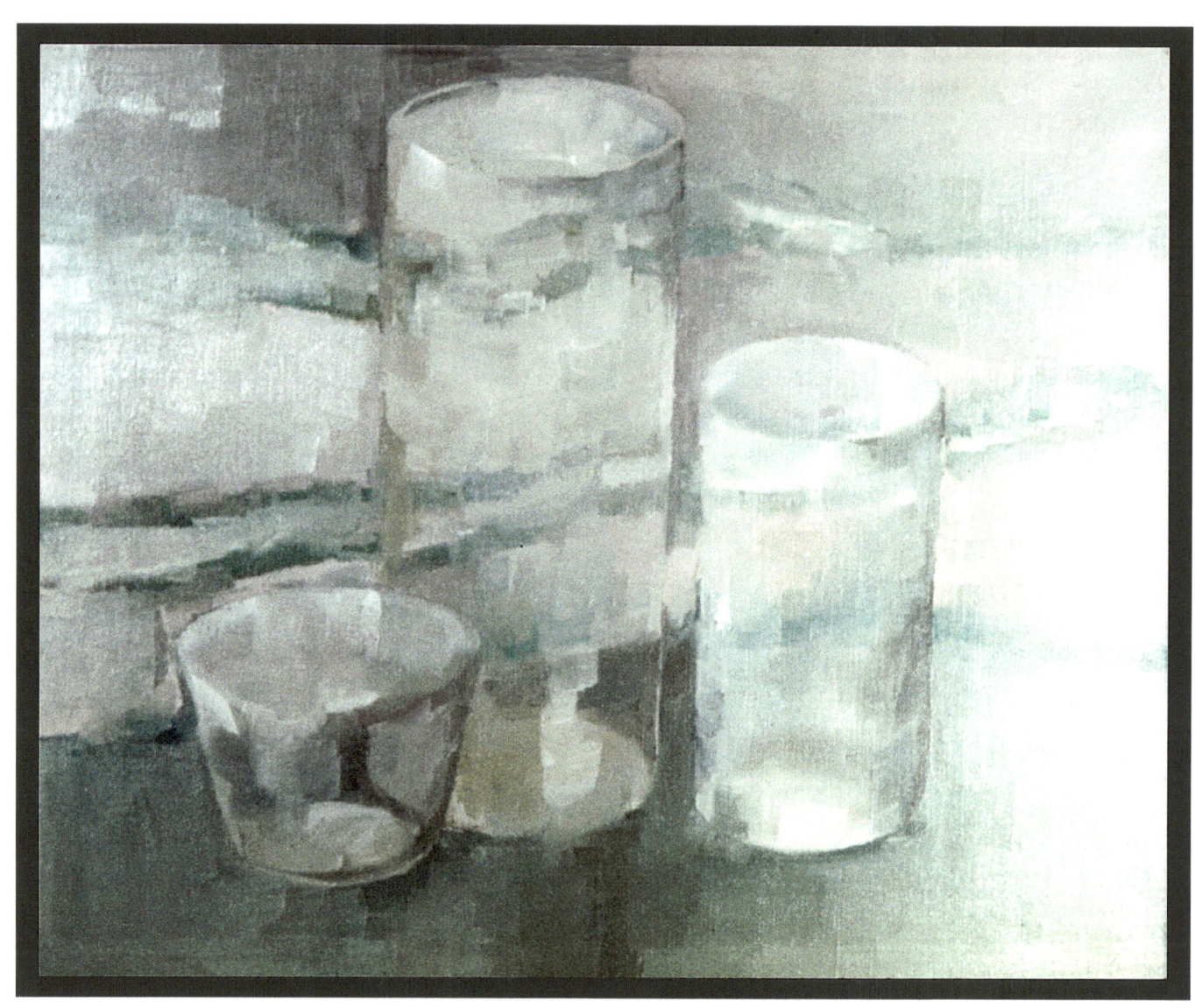

Three Glass Objects
Oil On Canvas

20

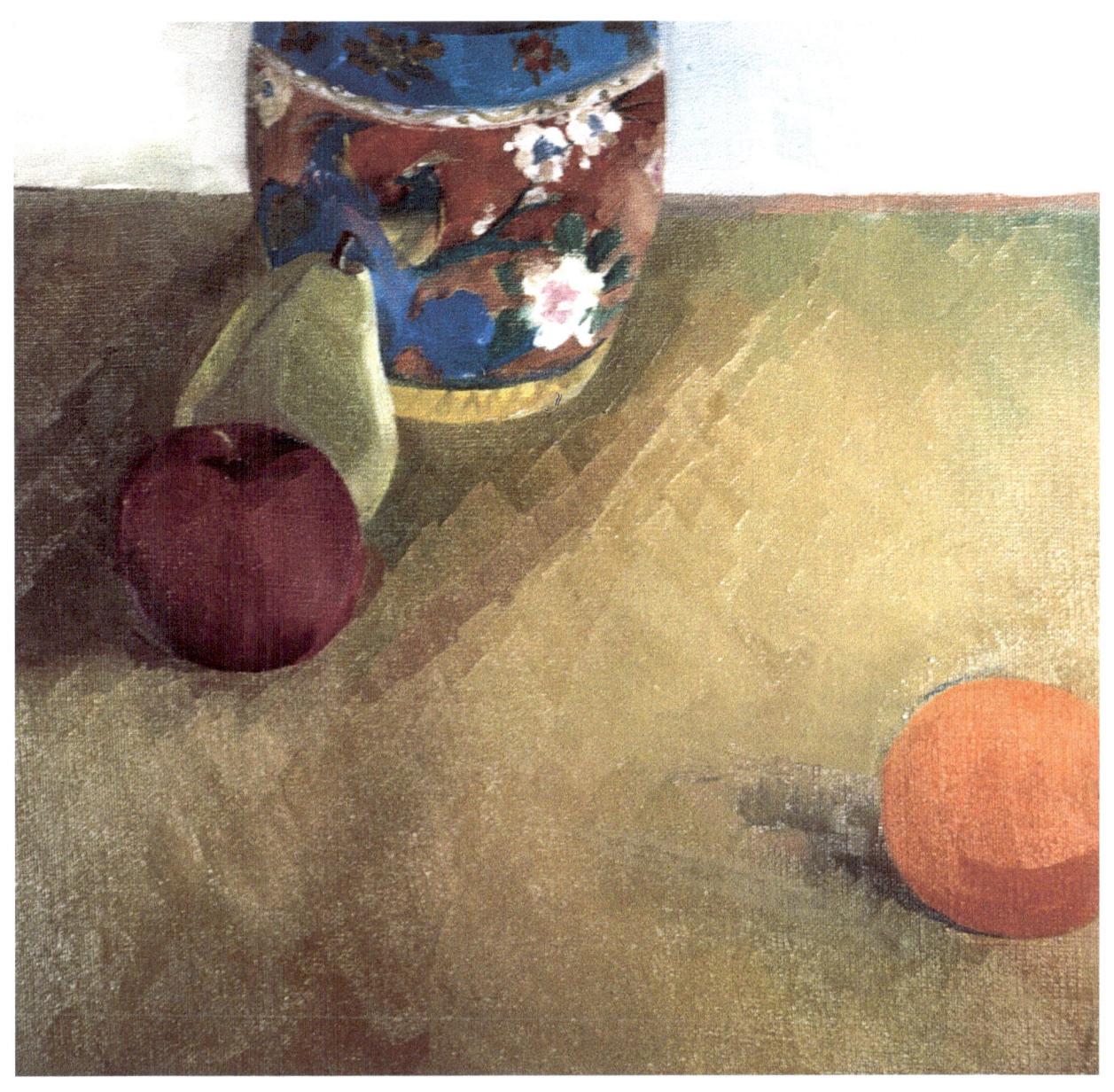

Japanese Vase
Oil on Canvas

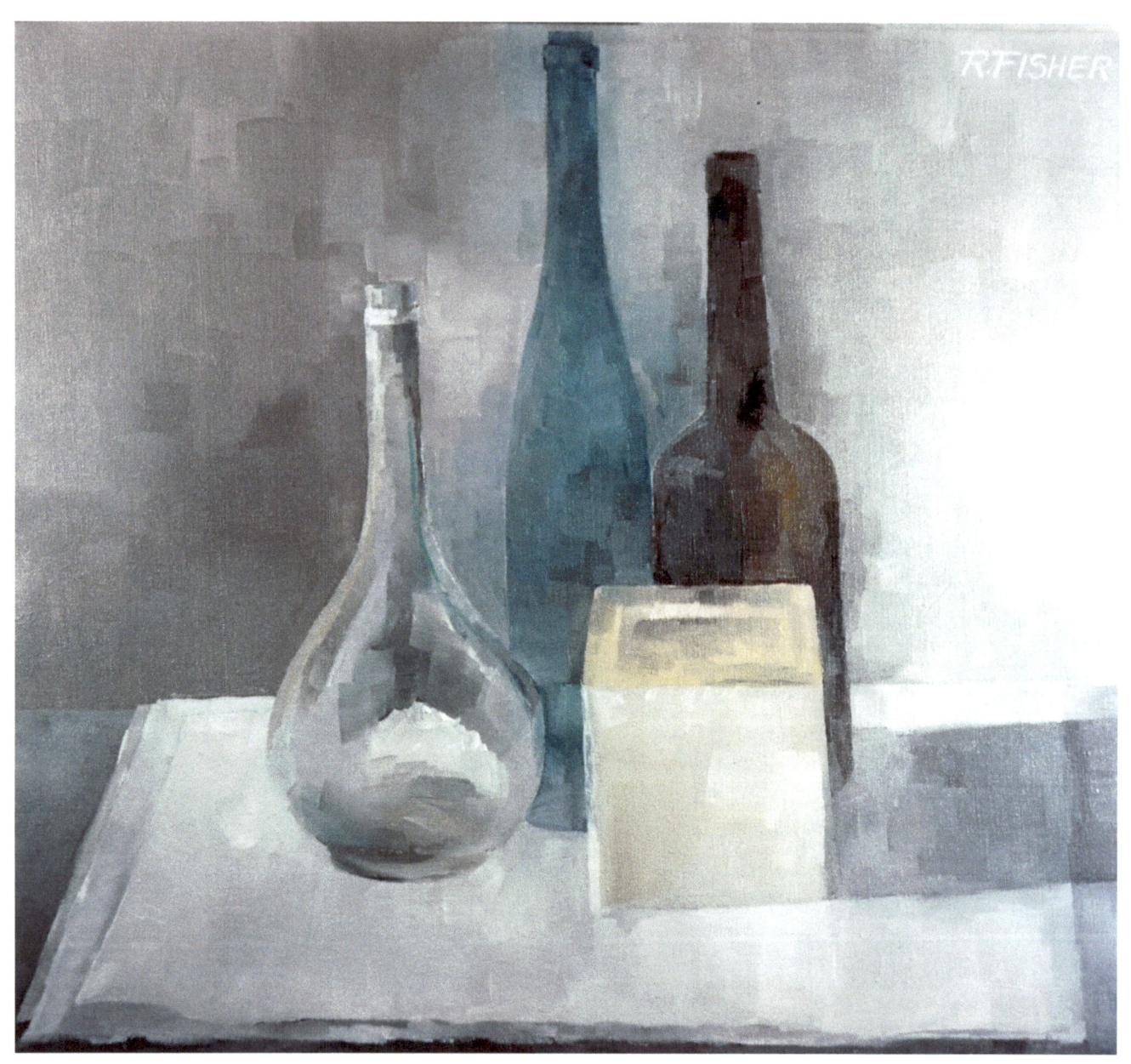

With Tea Canister
Oil on Canvas

22

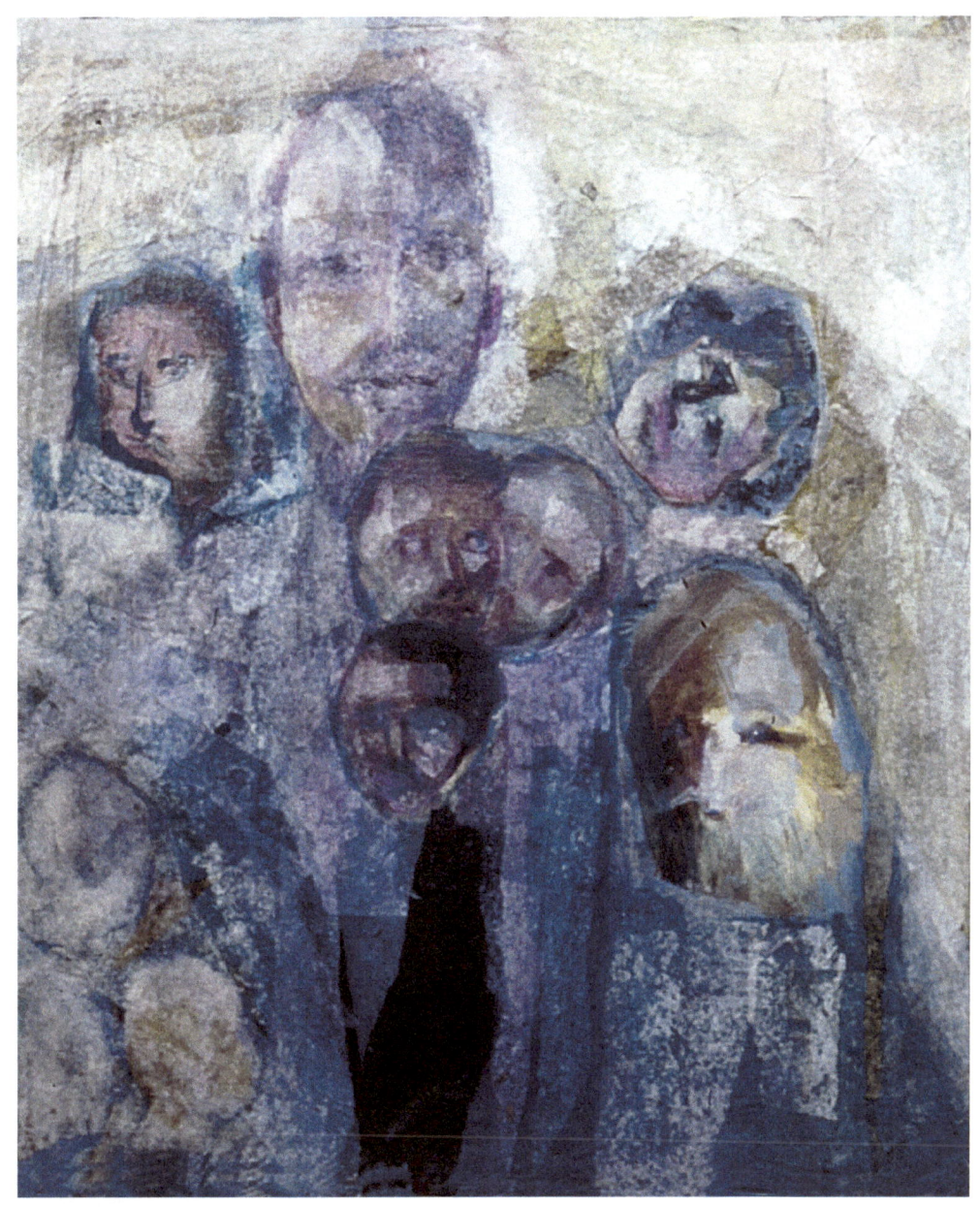

Around Me
Colored Tissue Paper
on Masonite

The second category of EARLY WORKS is *Figurative* images. Exploring different techniques and media is part of the challenge of visual imagery.

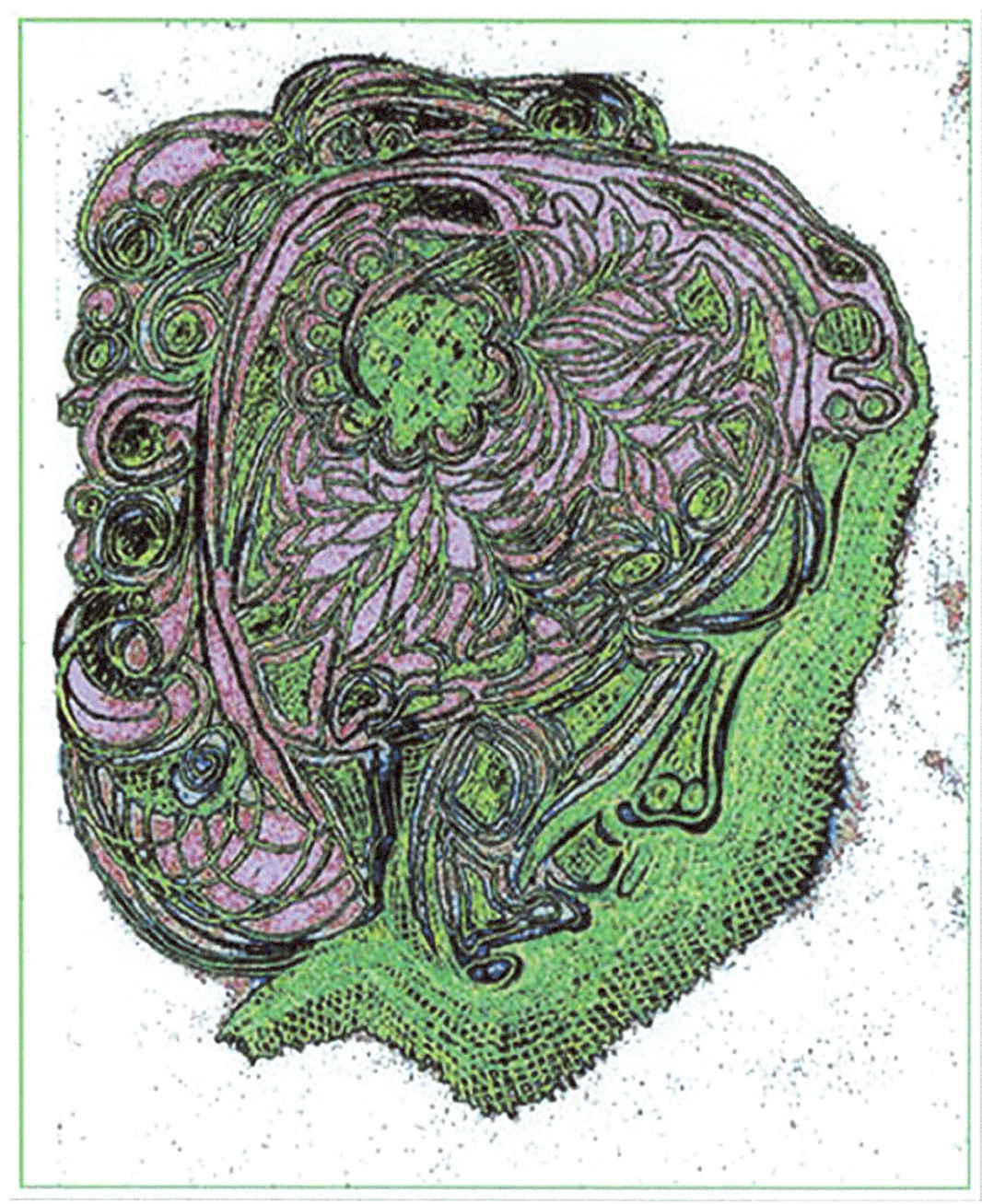

Polly

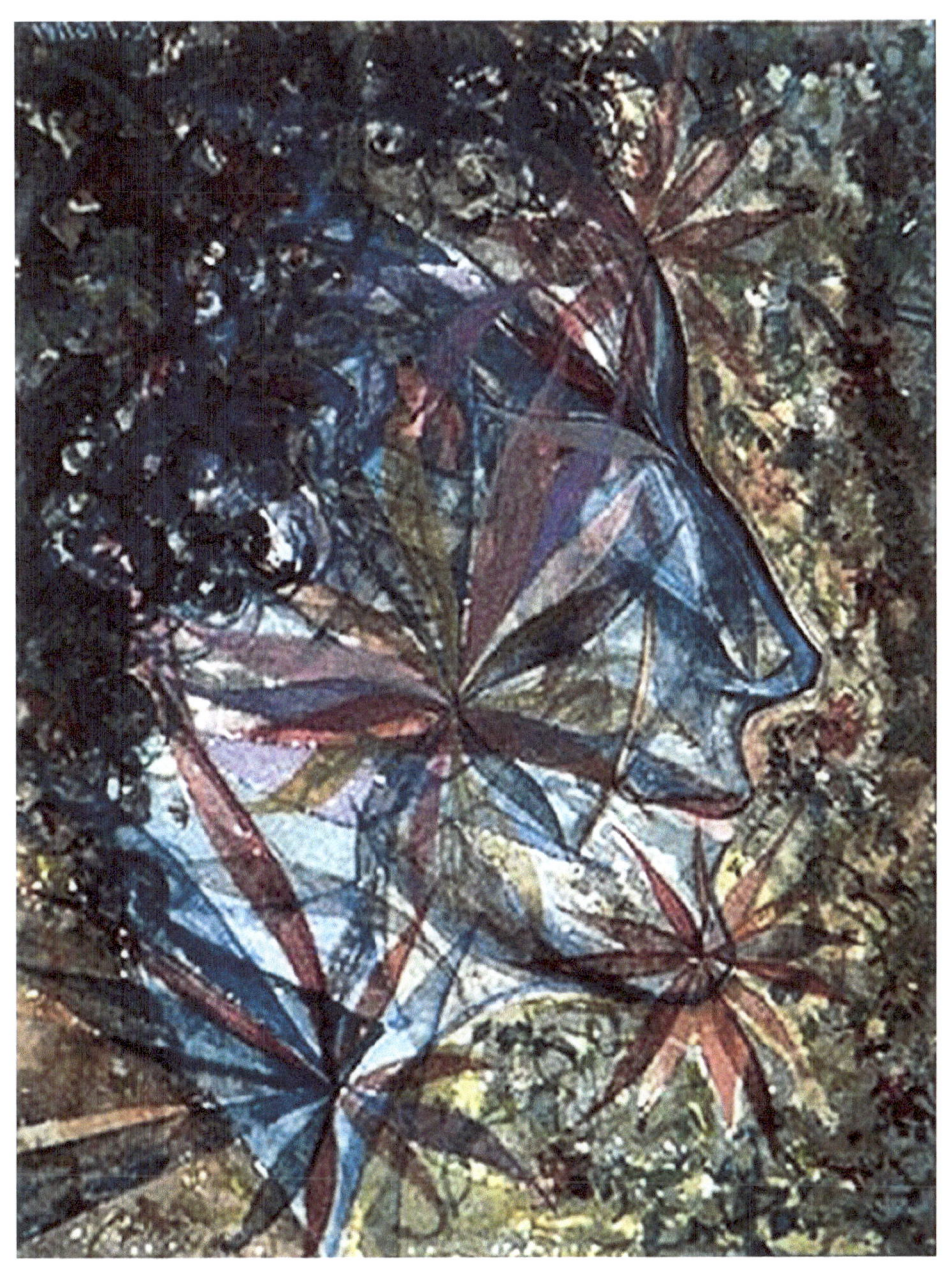

Eleanor
Gouache on Paper

25

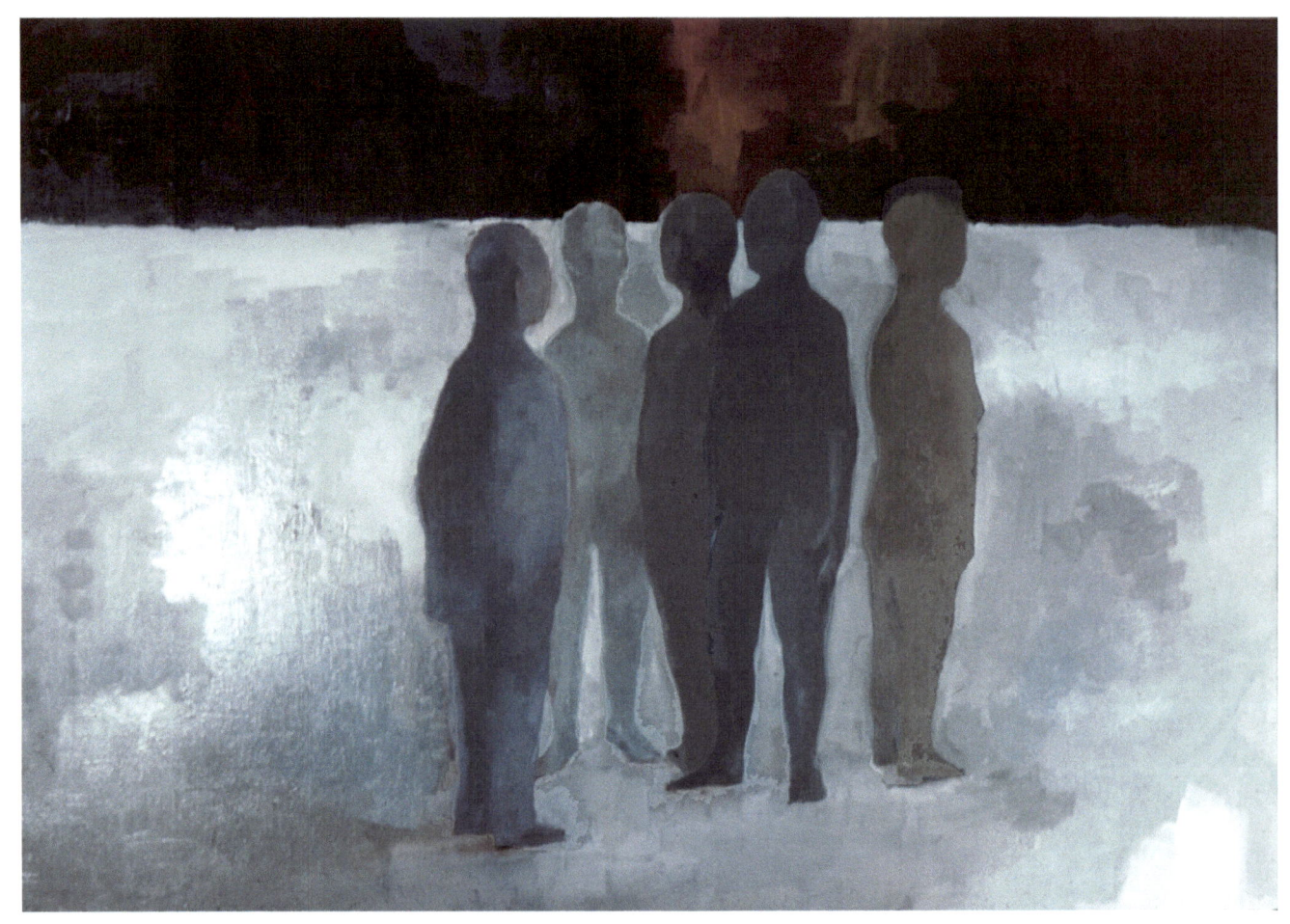

Identity Search
Oil on Canvas

Along with the *Self Portrait 1958*, this image was painted while a student of Reuben Tam at the Brooklyn Museum Art School.

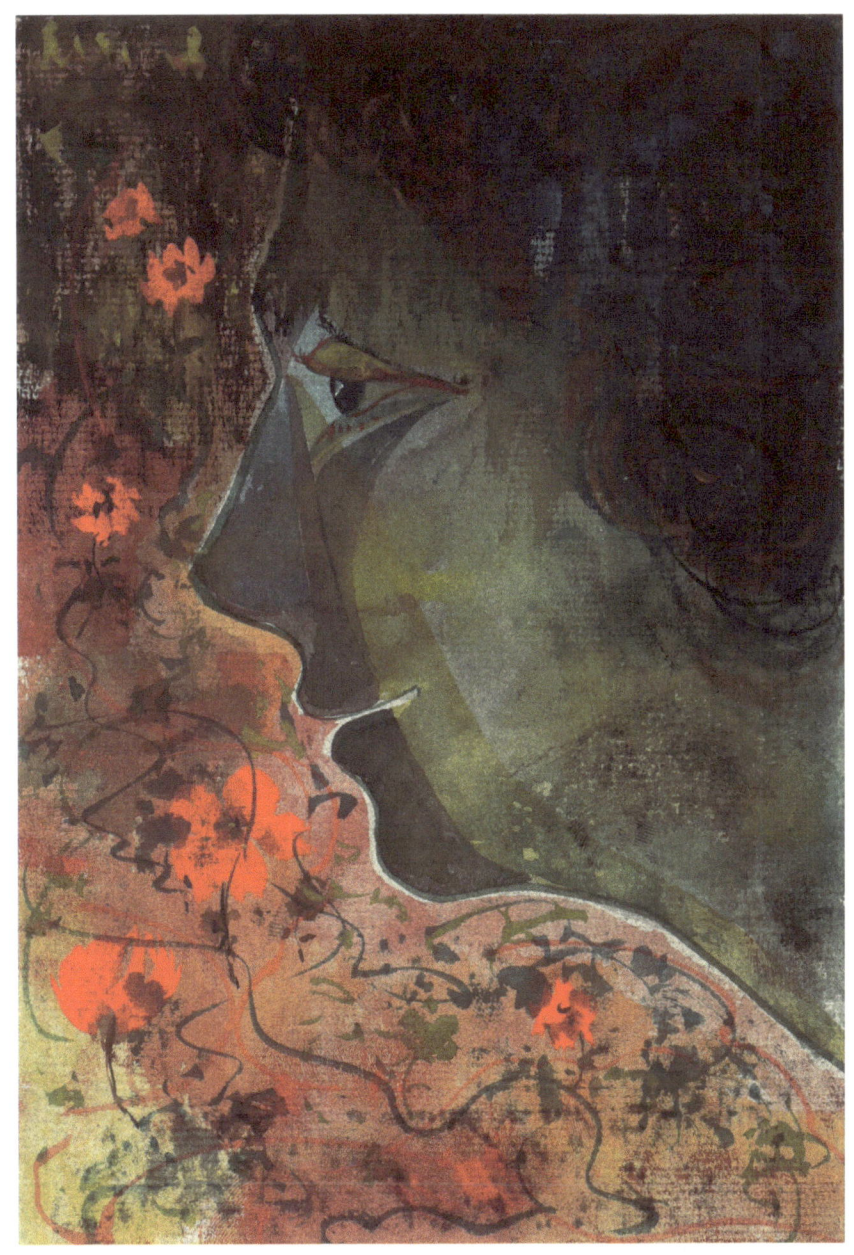

Sally
Gouache on Paper

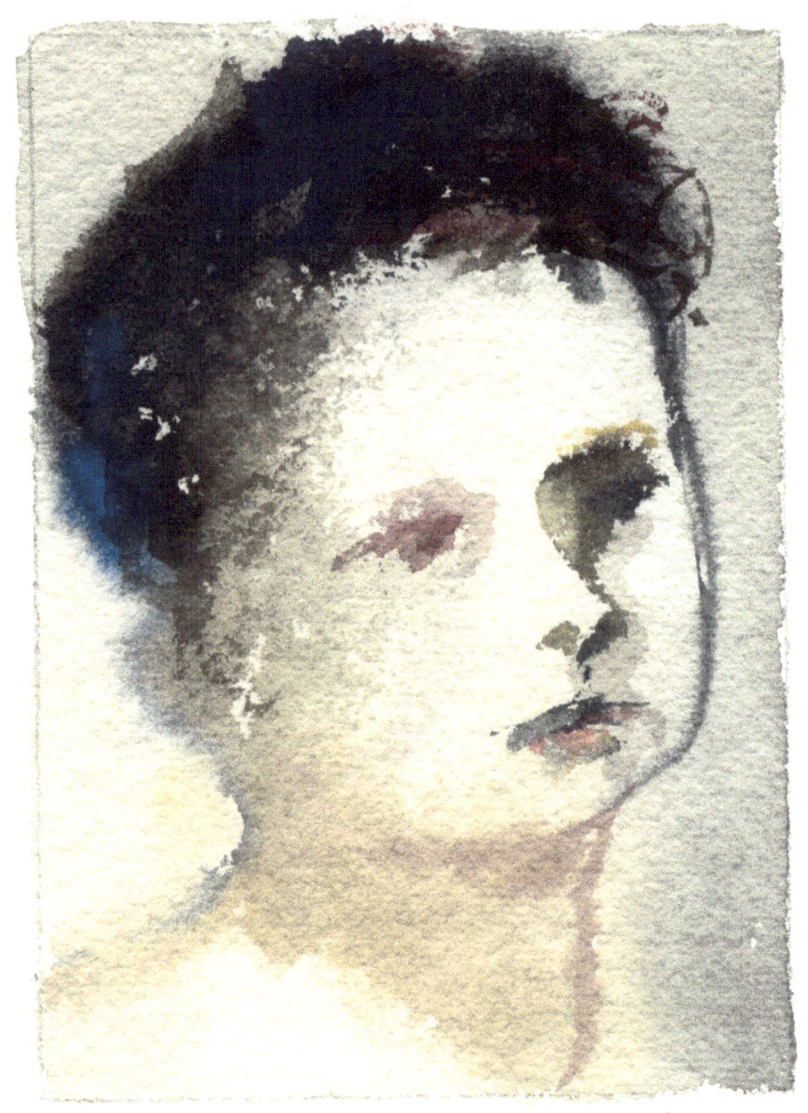

Woman's Face
Watercolor on Paper

28

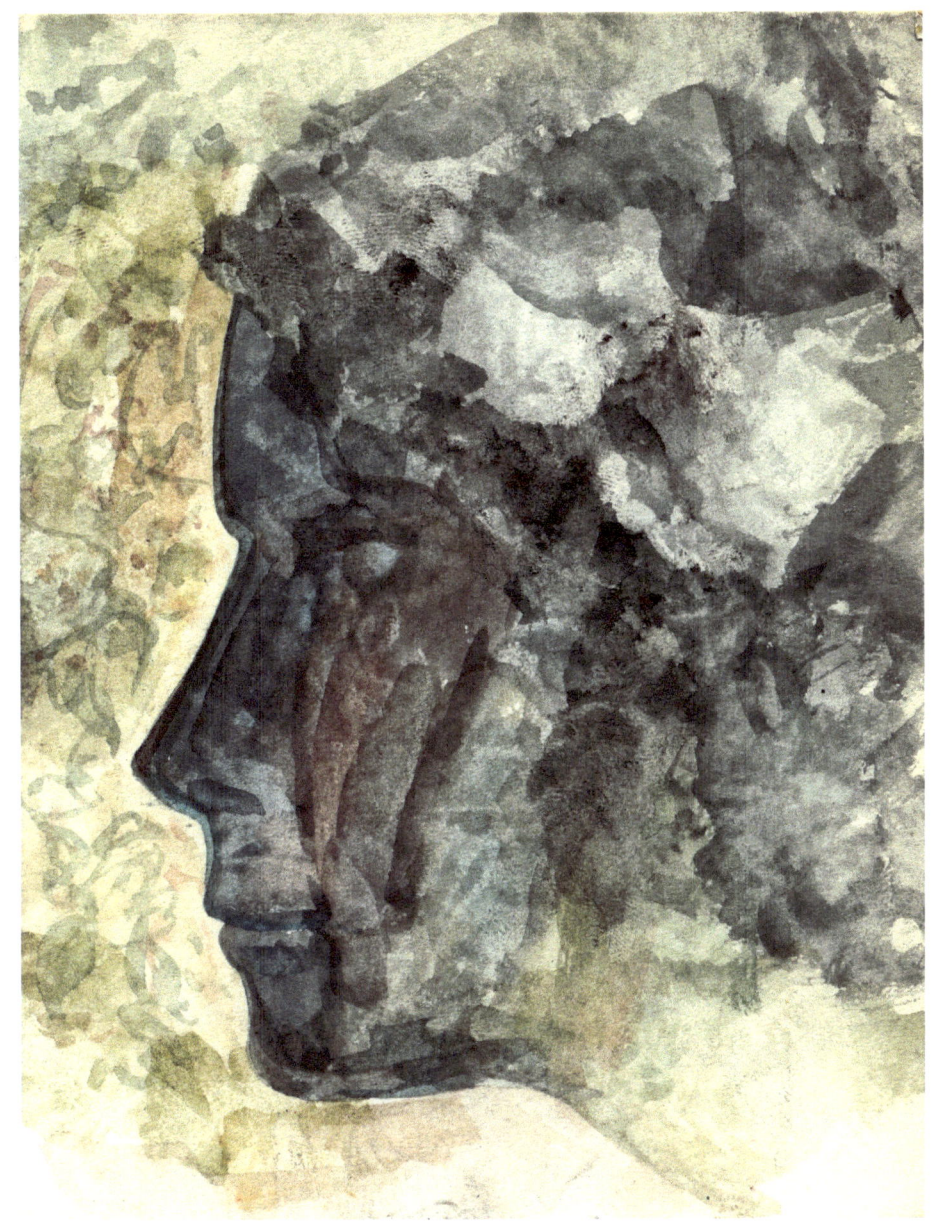

Head of a Girl
Gouache on Paper

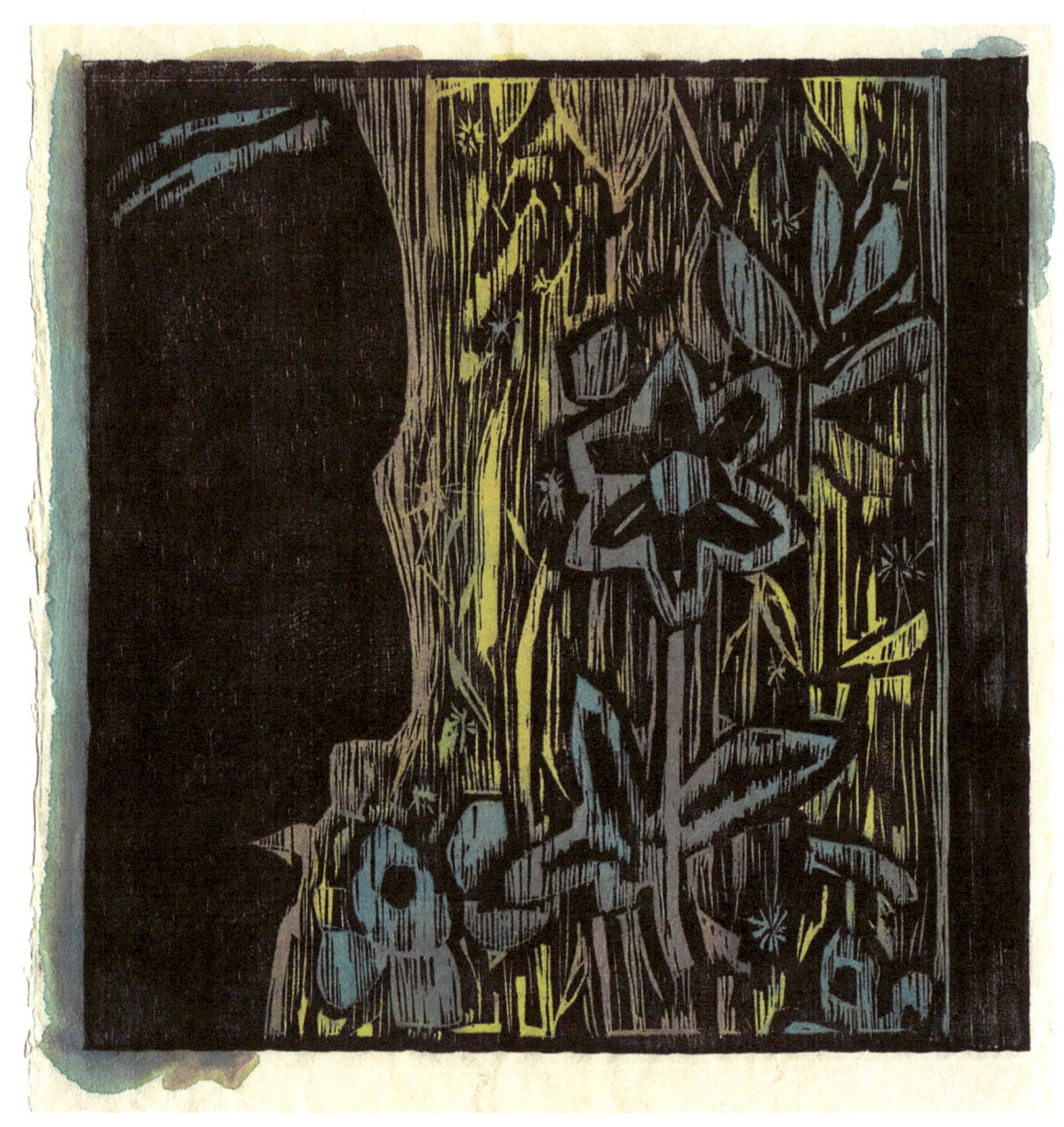

Homage to Redon
Woodblock Print on RicePaper
Enhanced with watercolors

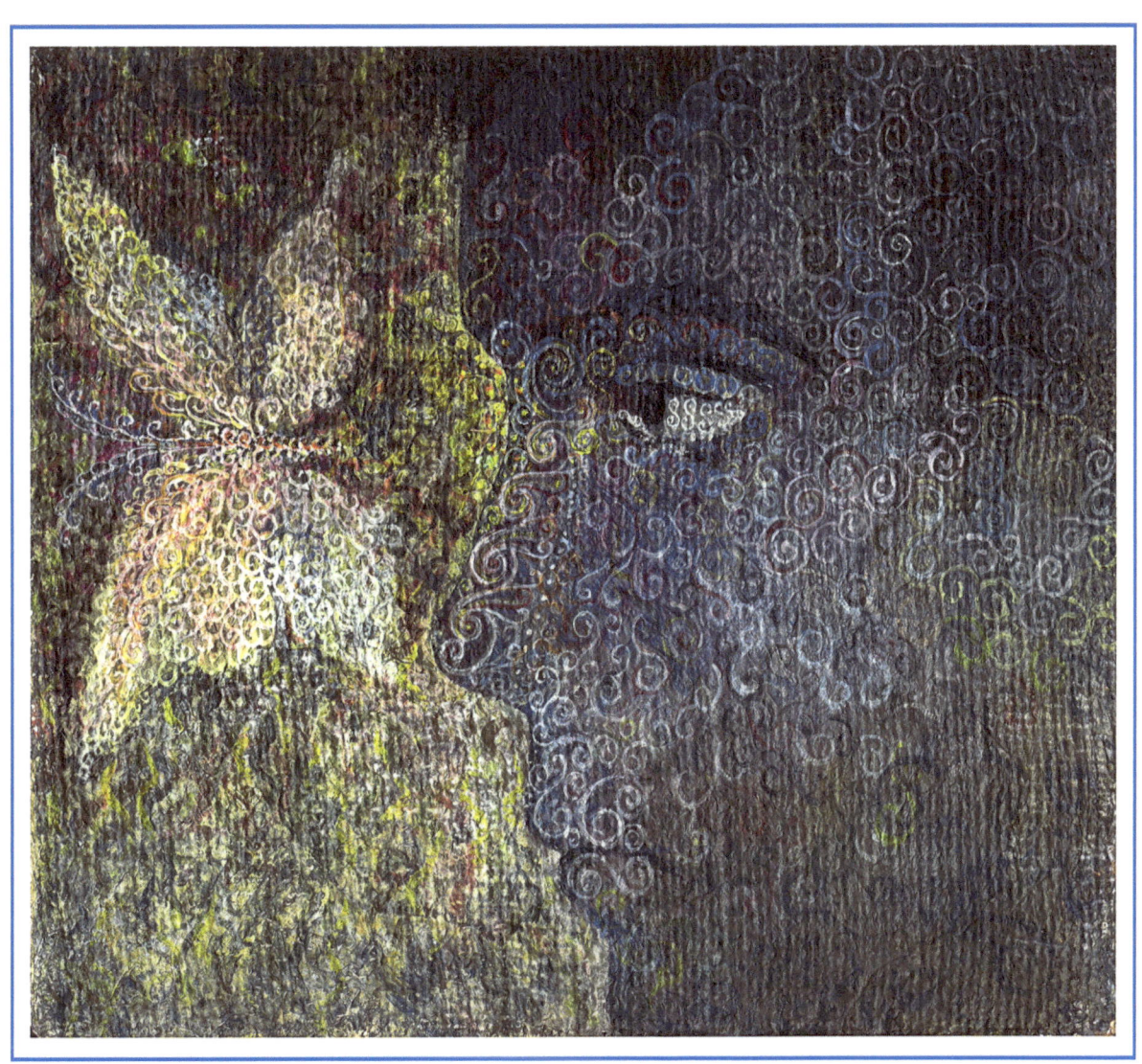

Luddy
Oil on Canvas
1963

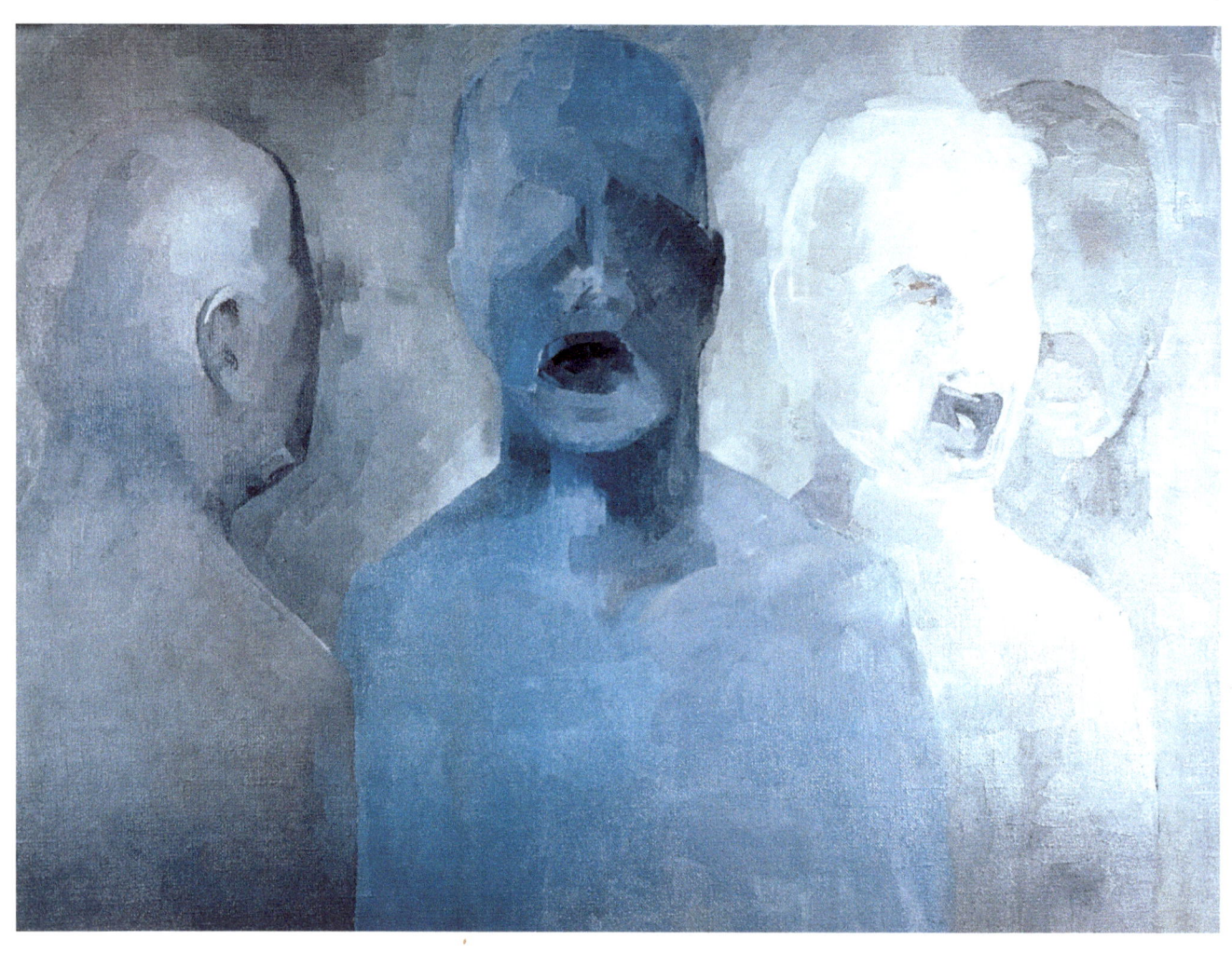

The Scream
Oil on Canvas

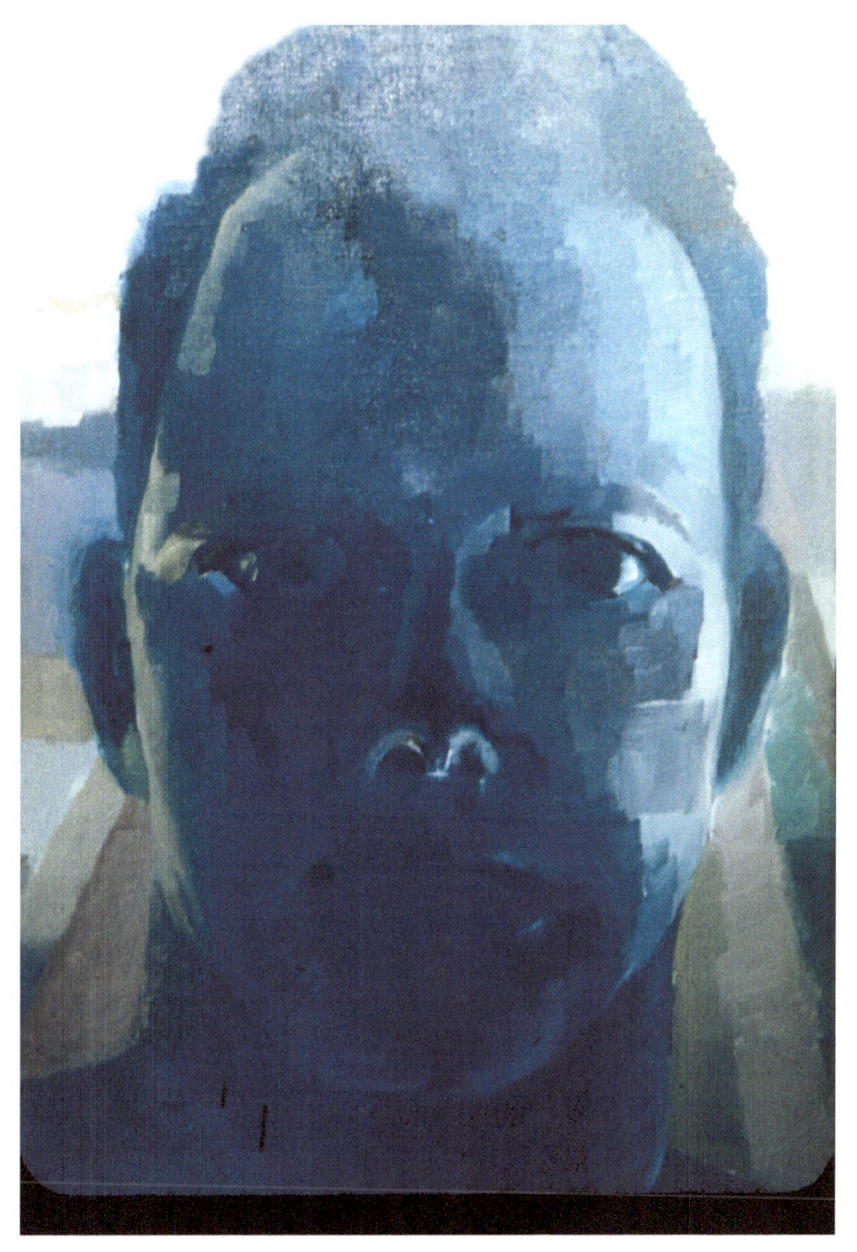

Self-Portrait
Oil on Canvas
1958

This is an early work while a
student at the Brooklyn Museum
Art School

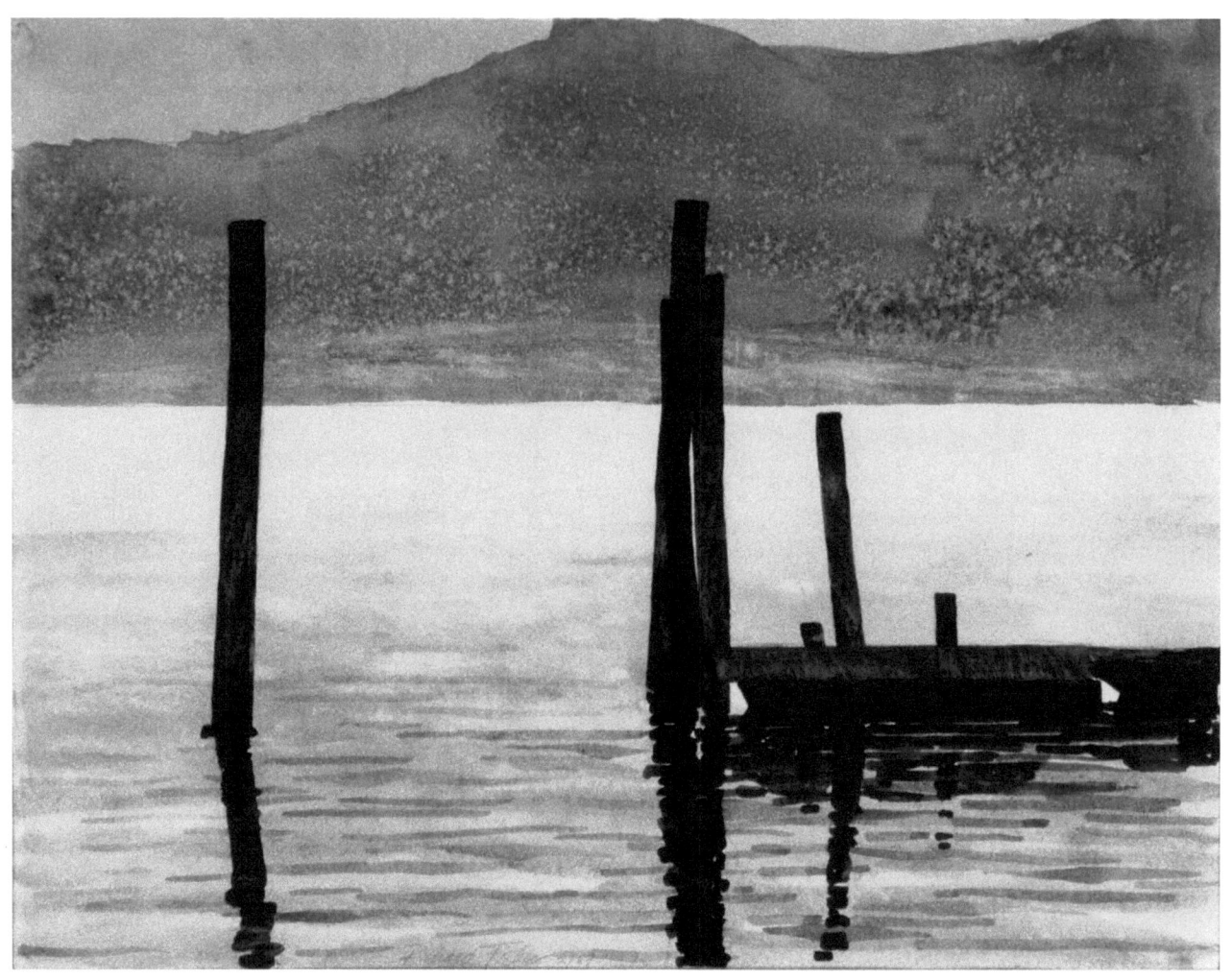

Hudson River Dock
Watercolor on Paper

The third category of EARLY WORKS is
Landscapes. The Hudson River Valley
produced many images.

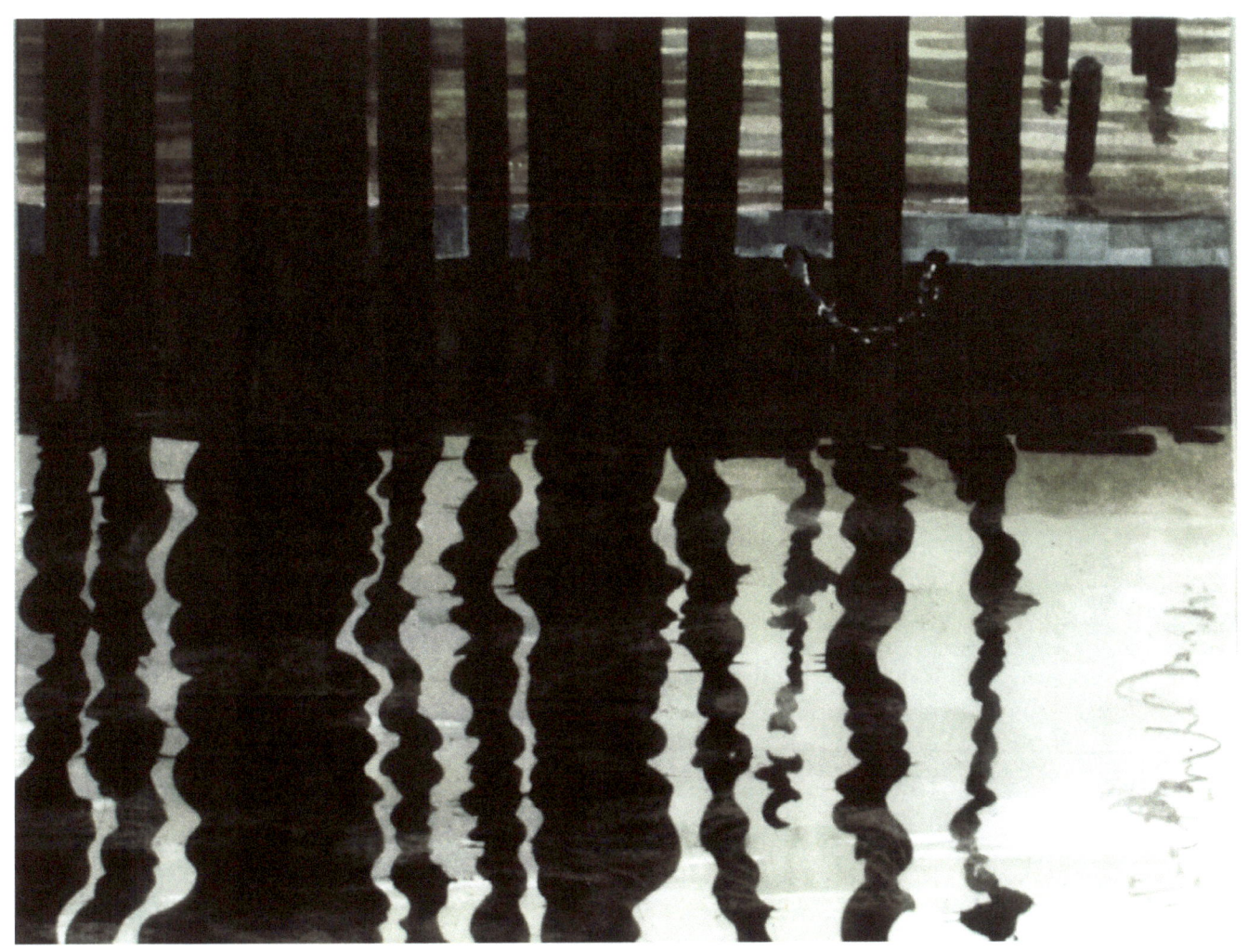

Dock Reflections
Watercolor on Paper

"Alone, without any reference to his
neighbors, without any interference,
the artist can fashion a beautiful
thing; and if he does not do it solely
for his own pleasure, he is not an
artist at all." ~OSCAR WILDE

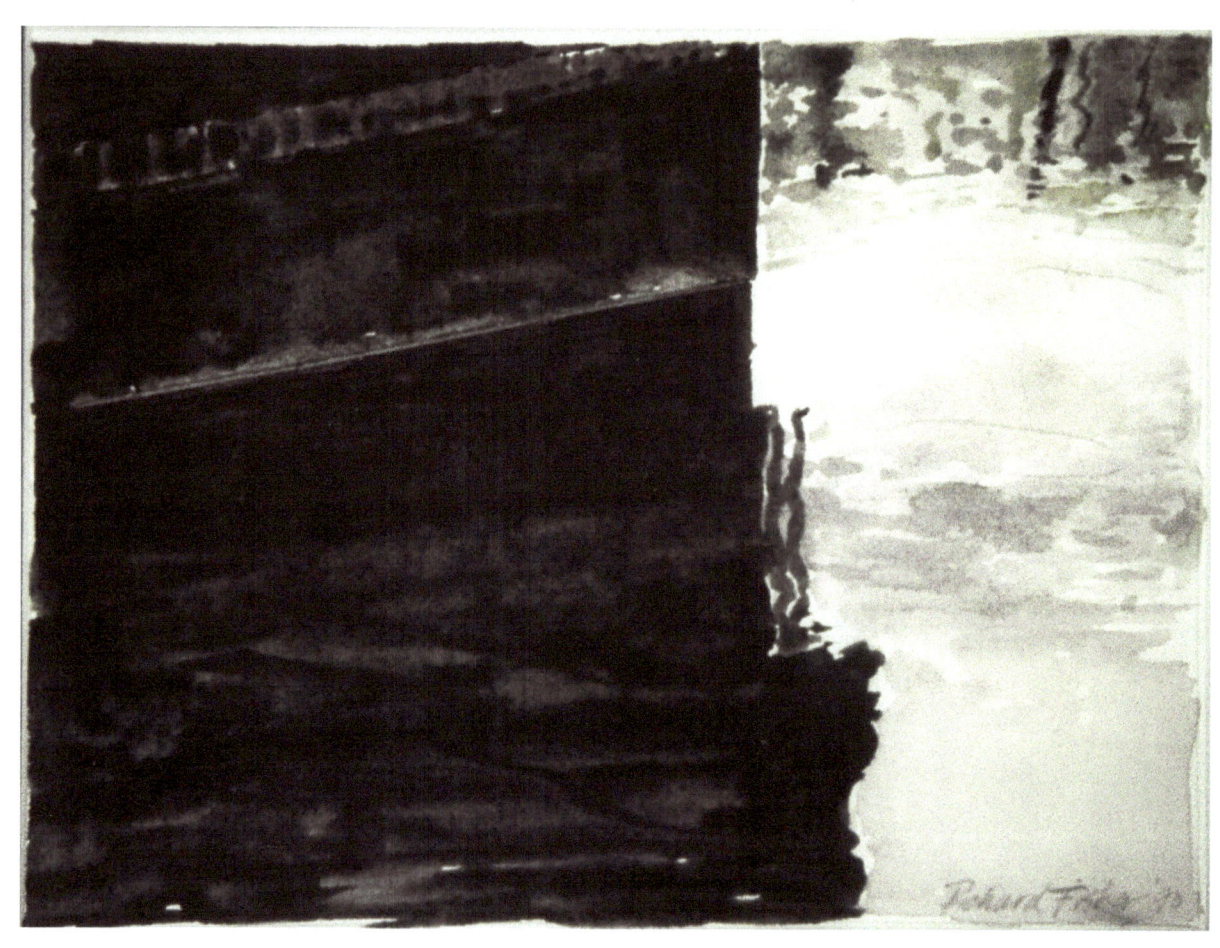

Marina Waters
Watercolor on Paper

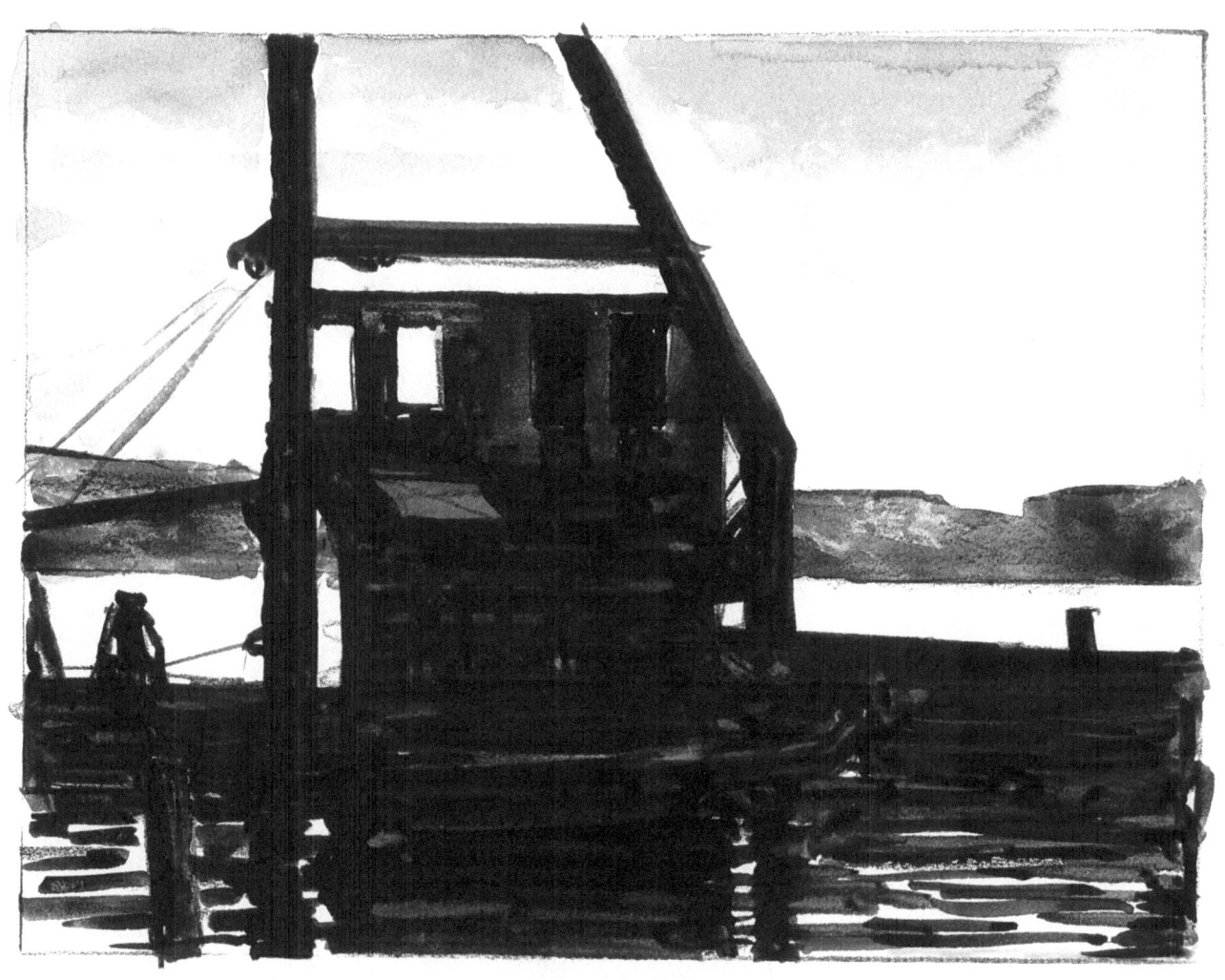

Derrick, Salty Dog Marina
Watercolor on Paper

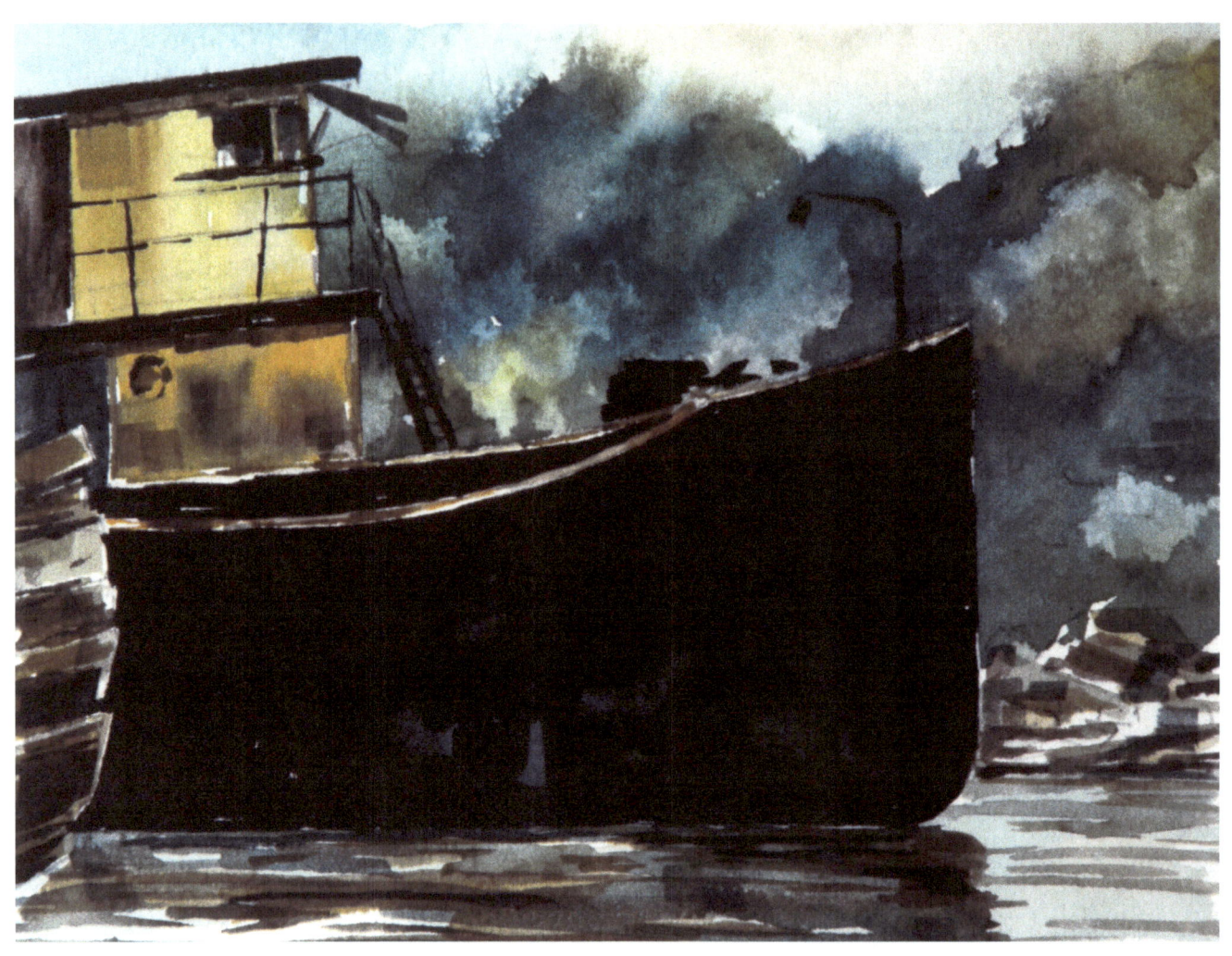

JoAnn's Tugboat
Watercolor on Paper

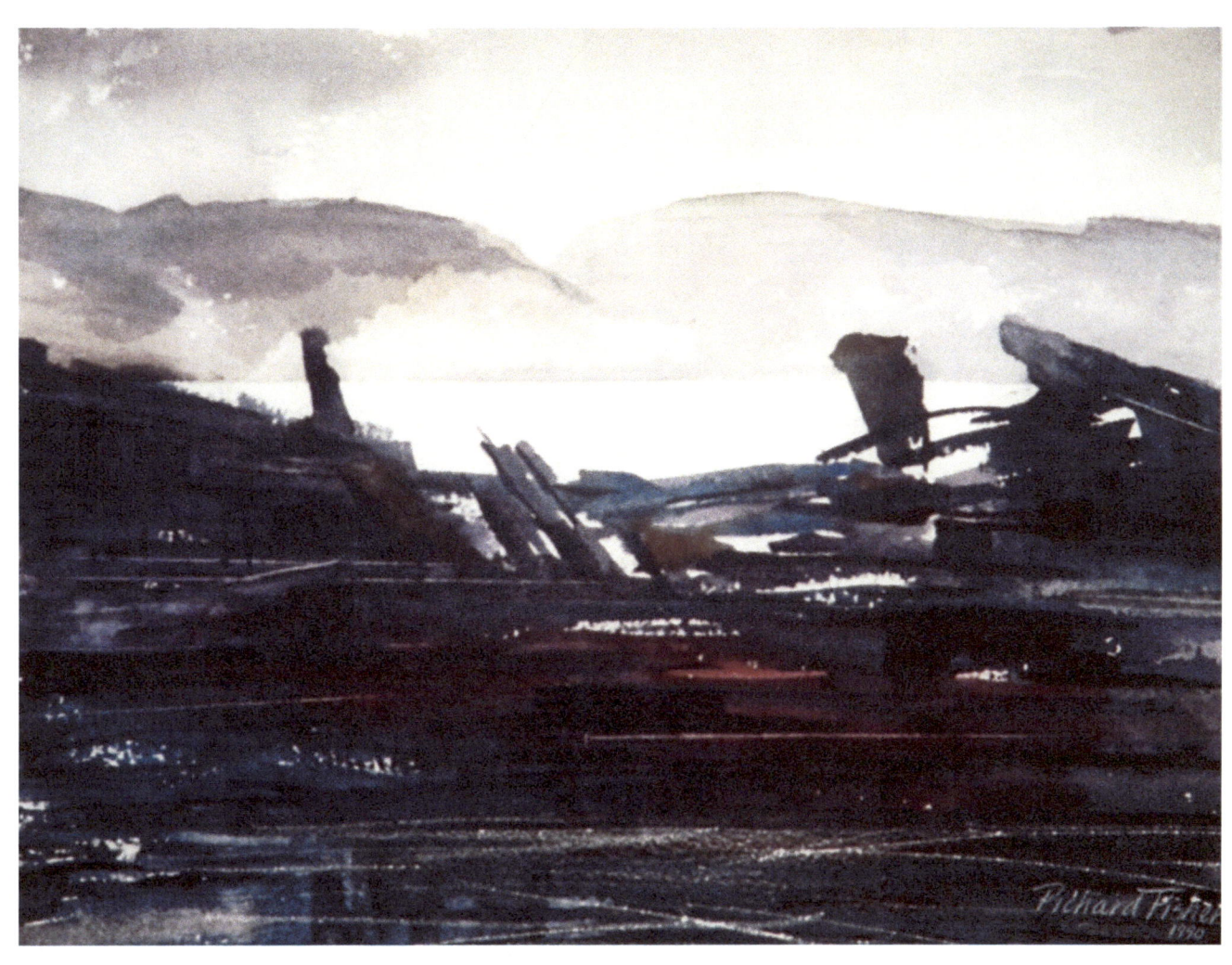

Barge Debris
Watercolor on Paper

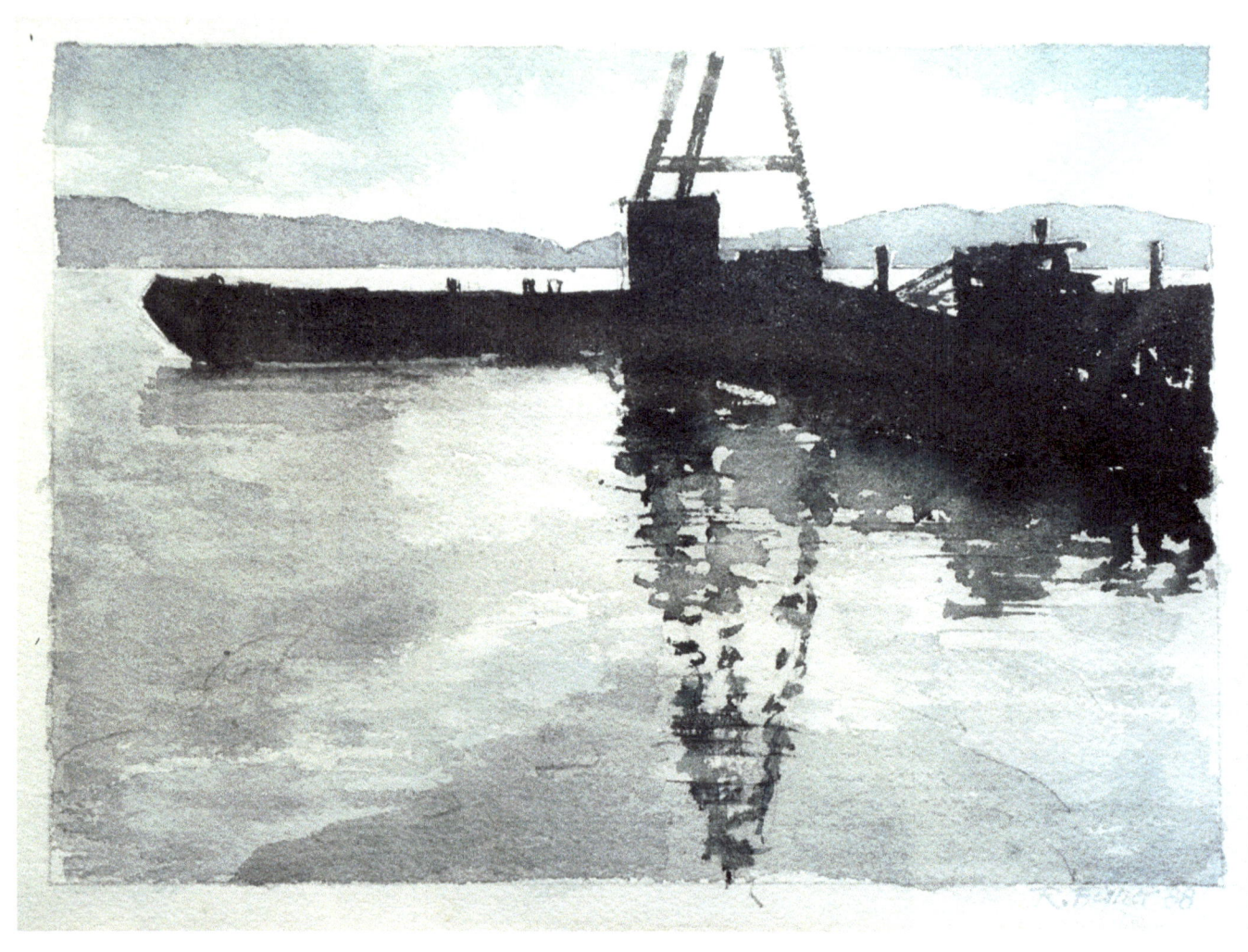

Johnsen's View
Watercolor on Paper

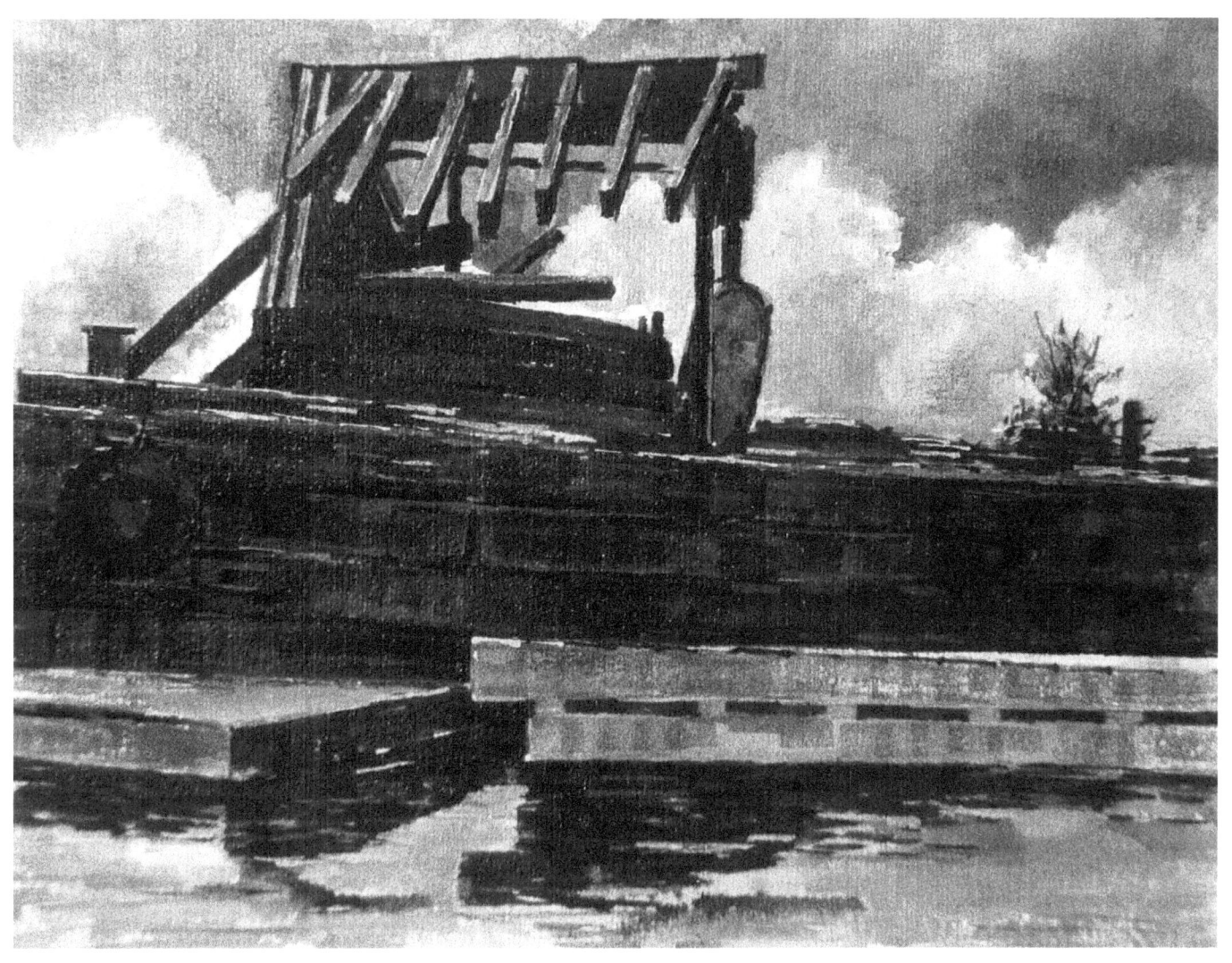

Barge, Salty Dog Marina
Watercolor on Paper

The Salty Dog Marina is in Verplanck, NY
on the Hudson River. Old barges were
sunk into the mud to protect the marina
from the action of waves caused by wind
and weather and passing tankers.

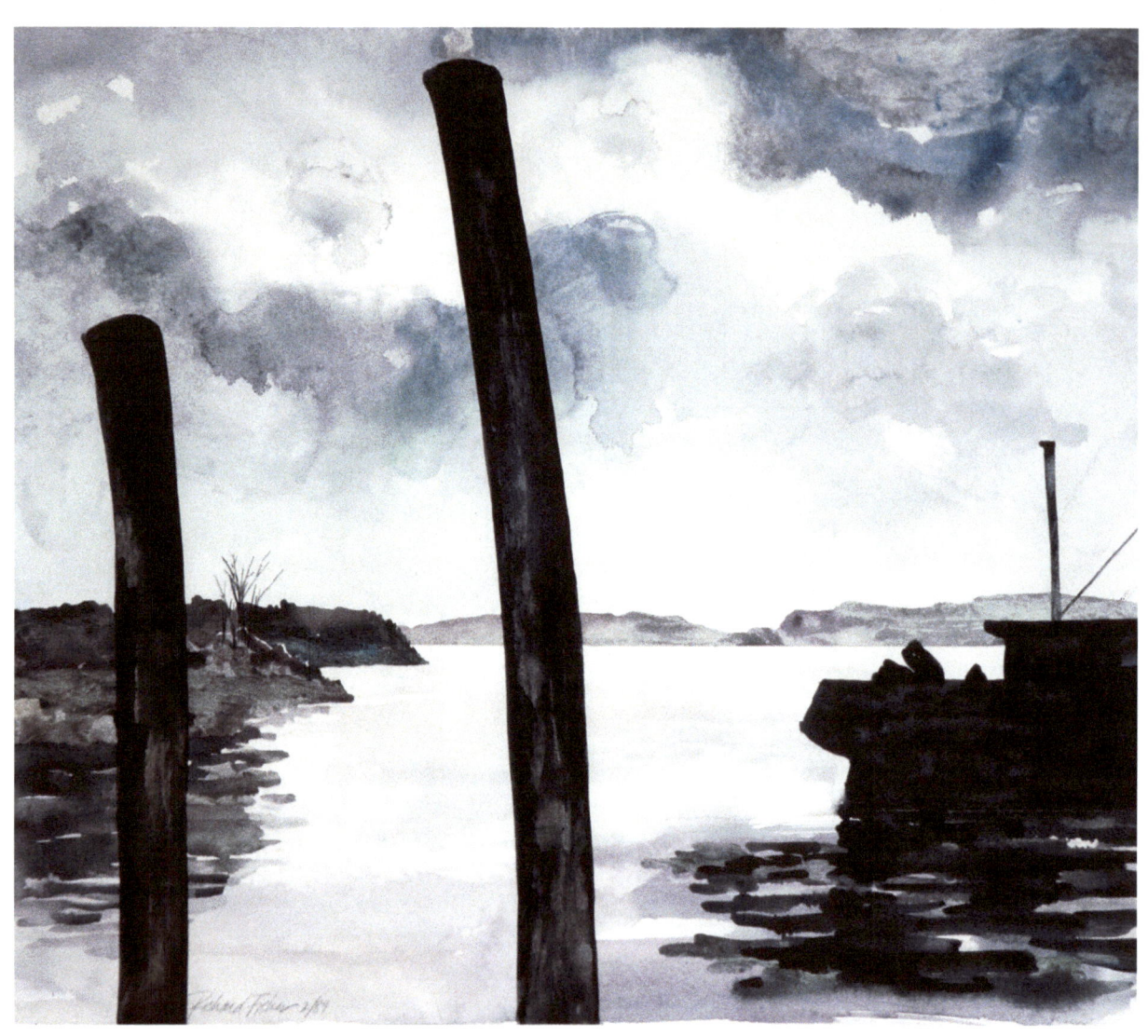

Verplanck on the Hudson
Watercolor on Paper

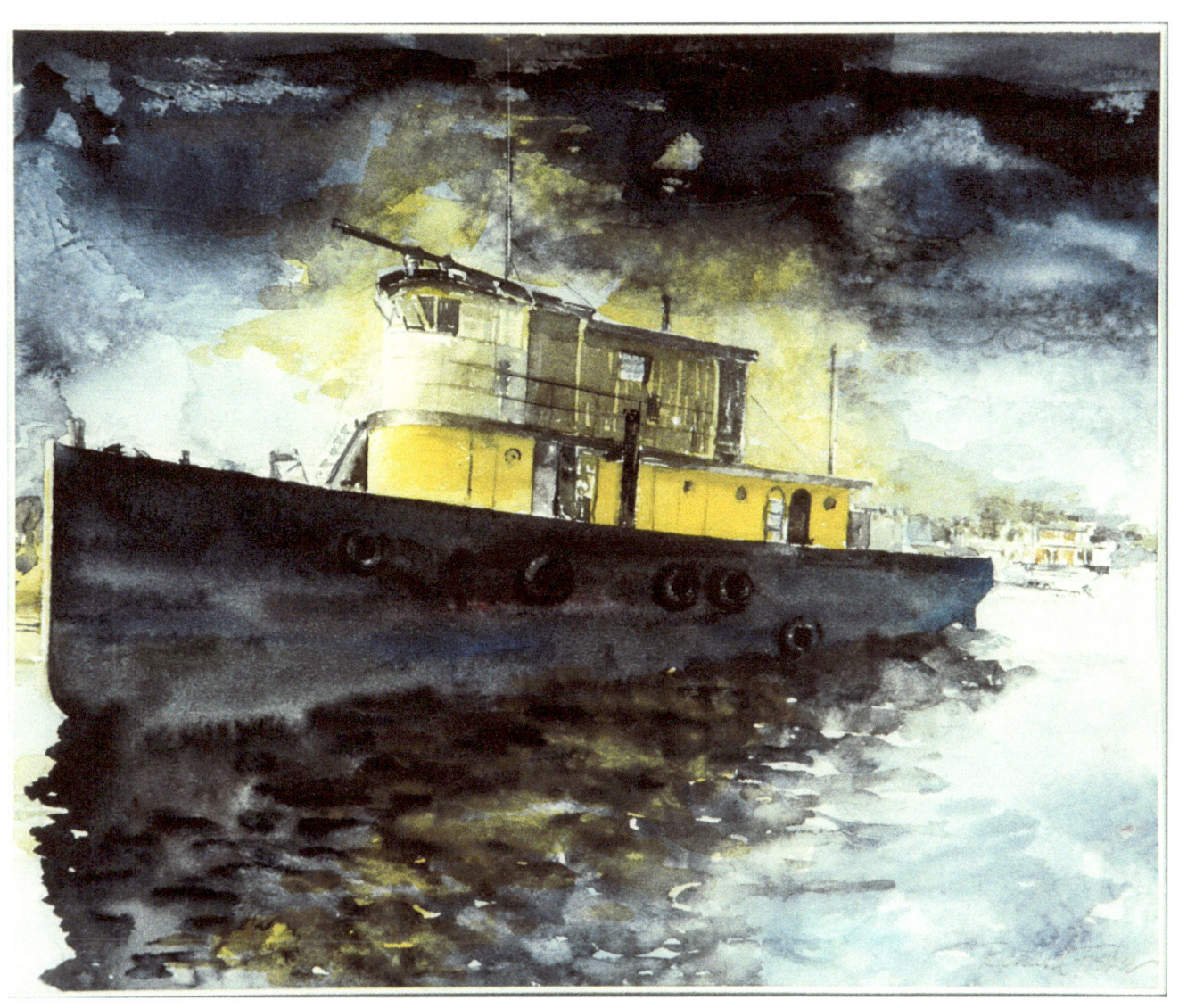

William's Tug in Verplanck
Watercolor Commission

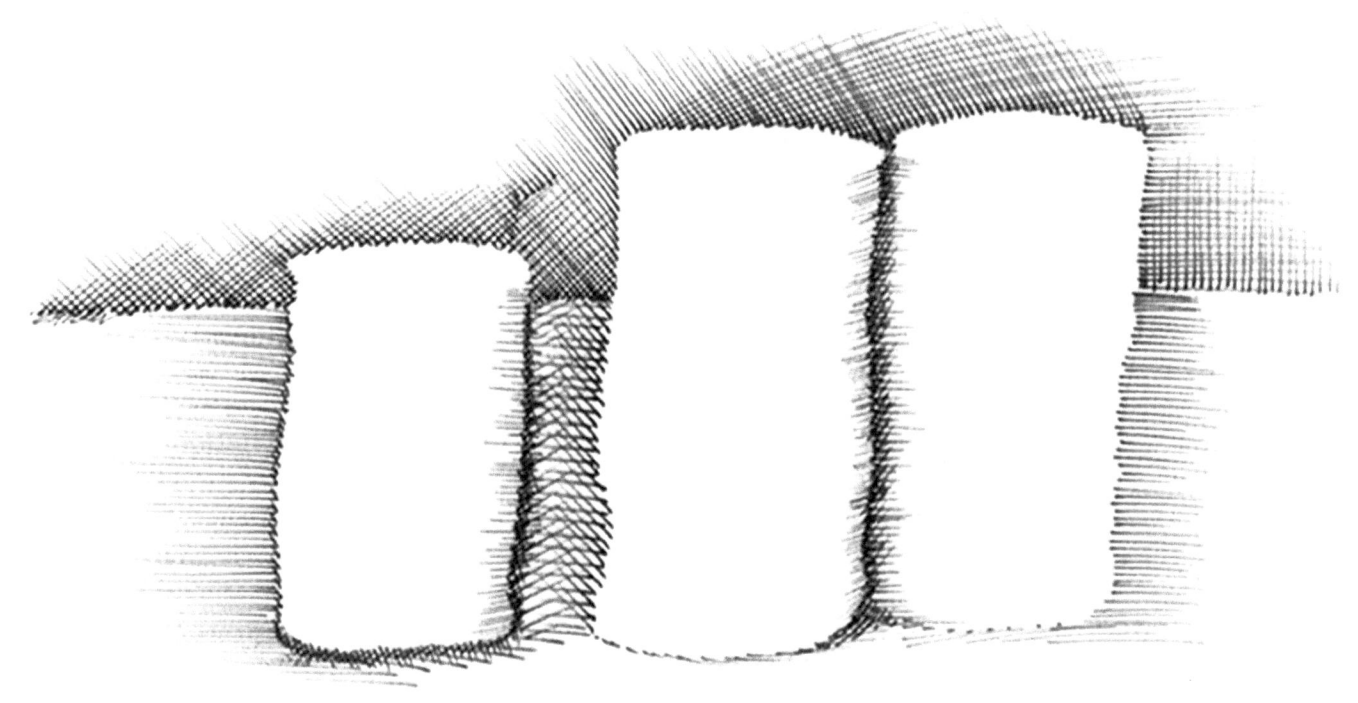

Three Tins
Black Marker on Paper

The fourth category of EARLY
WORKS is *Sketchbook*, a few images
selected at random.

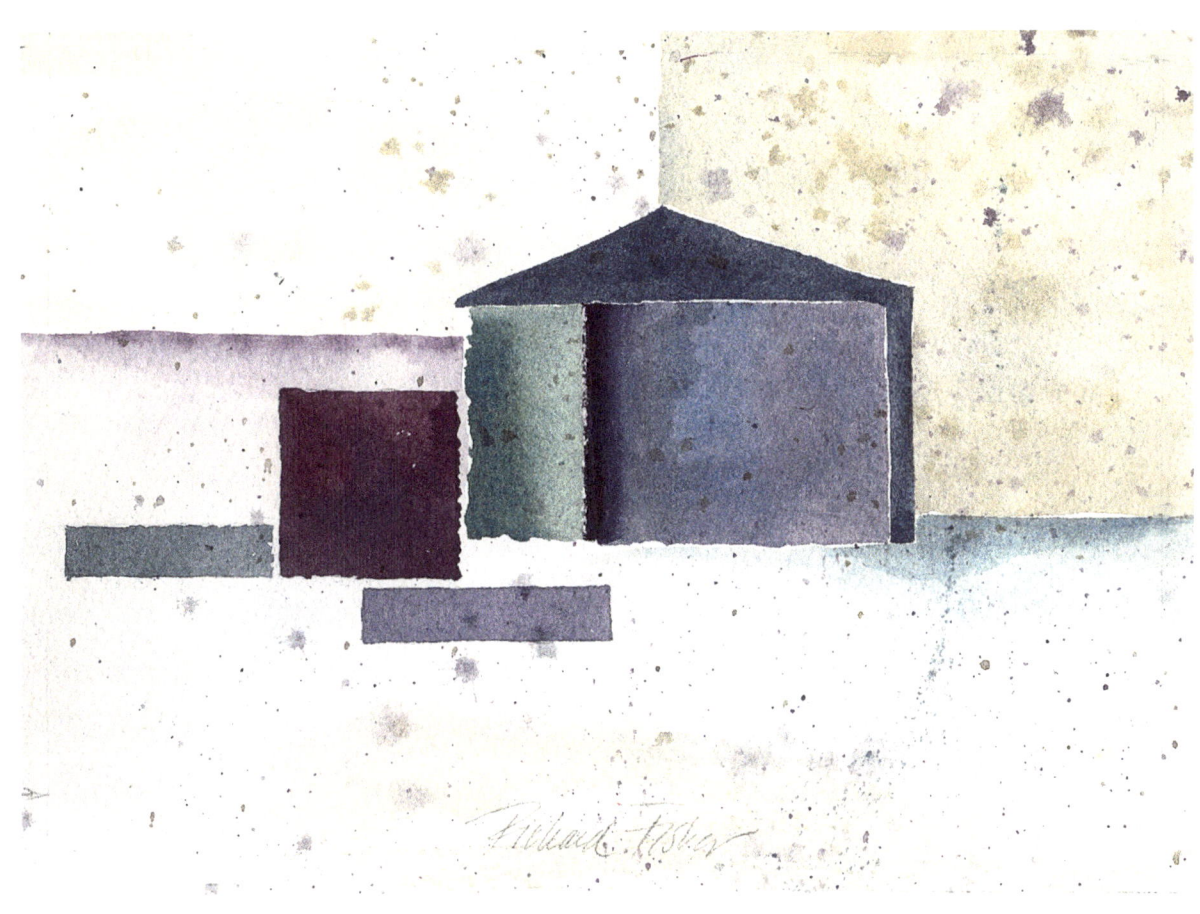

Buildings
Watercolor on Paper

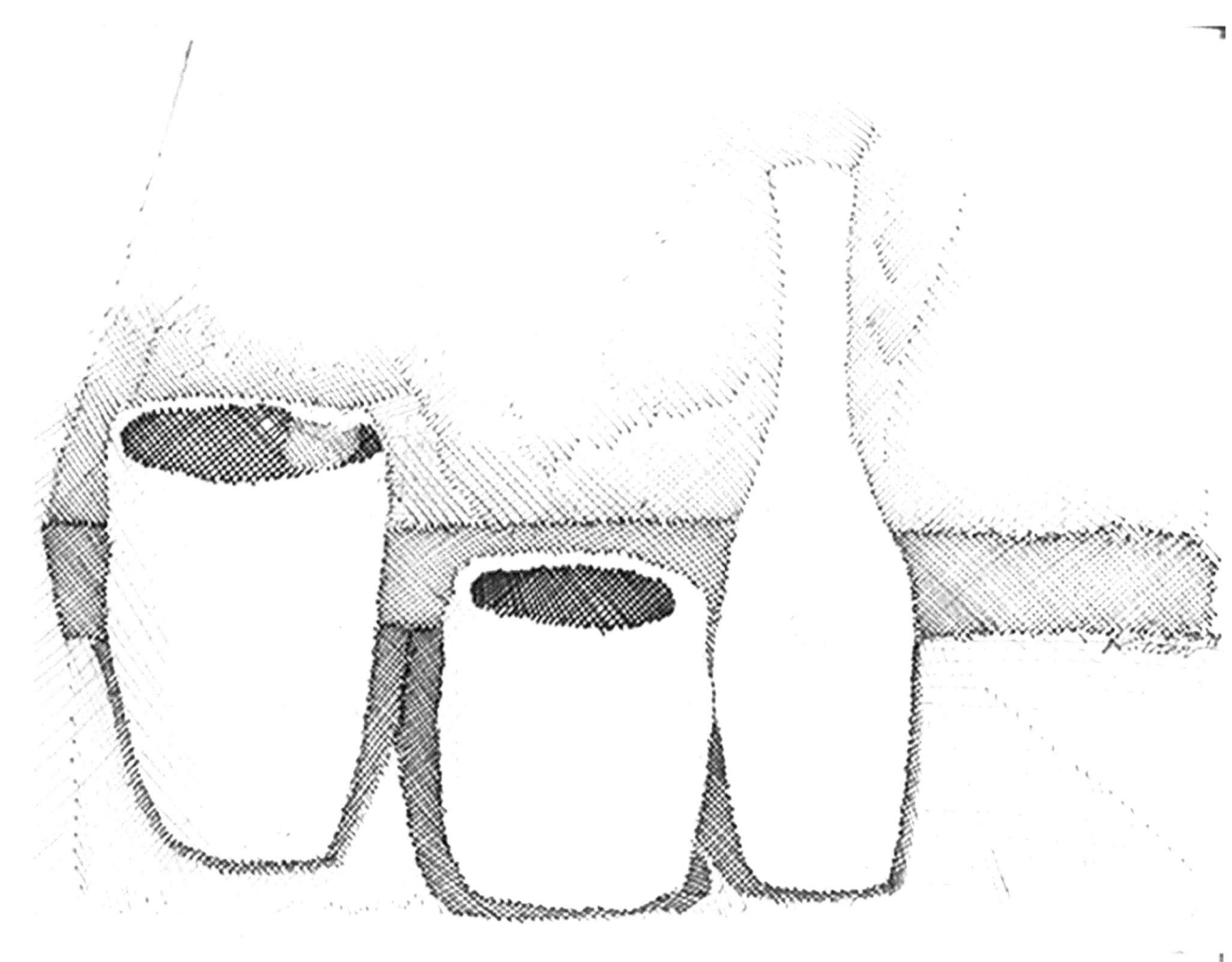

Two Pots & Vase
Black Marker on Paper

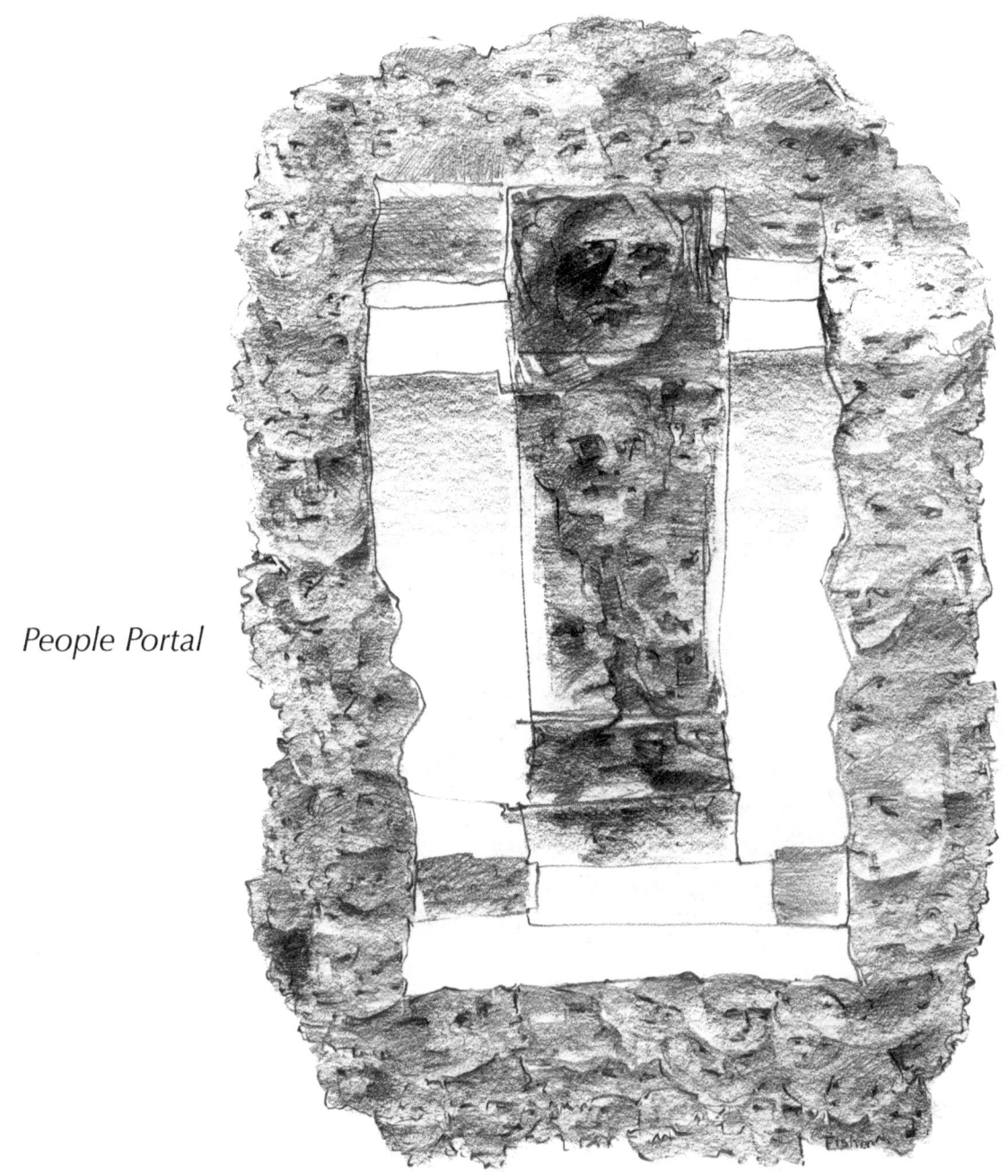

People Portal

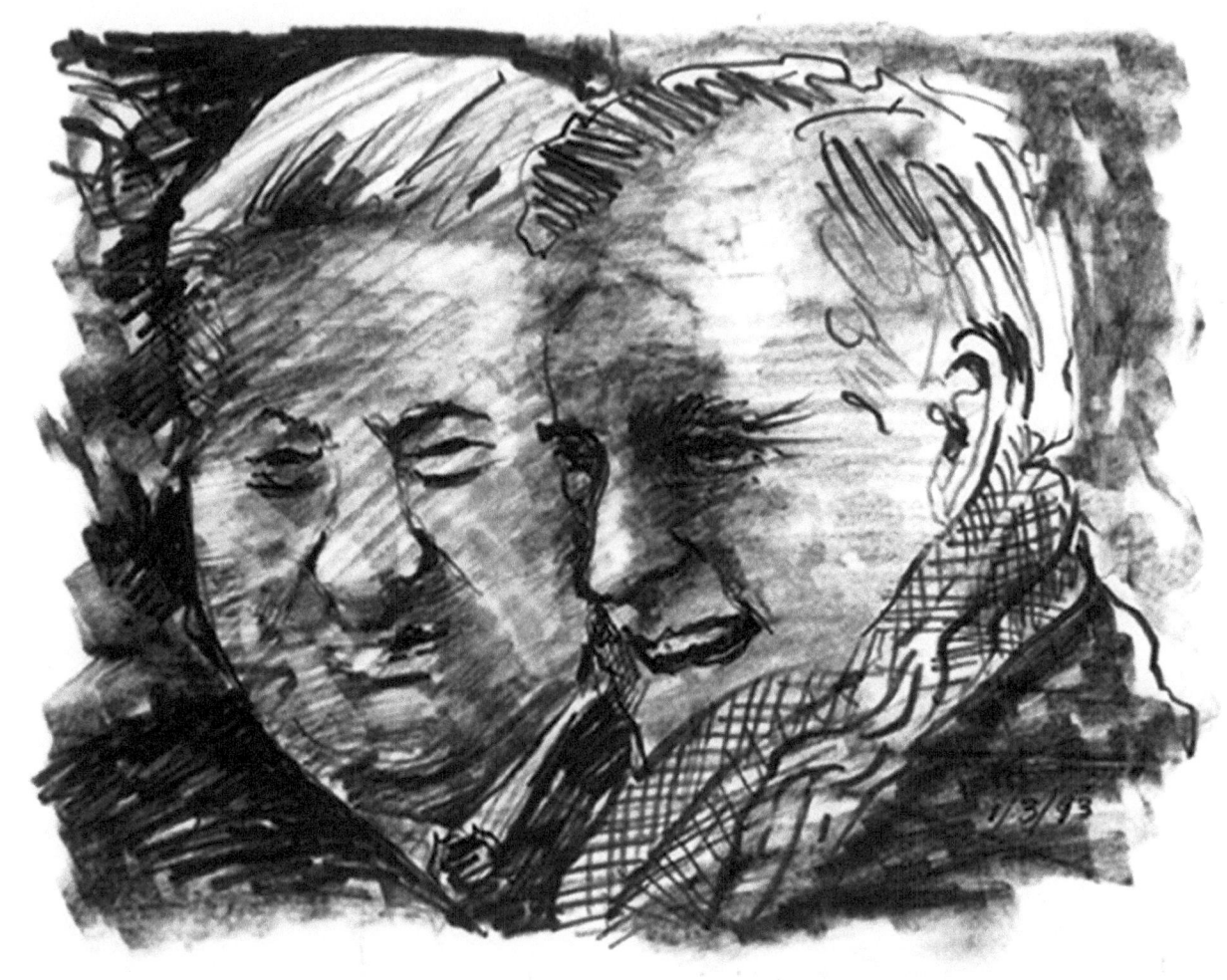

*Bush Sr. &
Nikita Khrushchev*
Graphite on Mylar Film

The first of several sketches
from Newspaper Photos
titled *The President Series*.

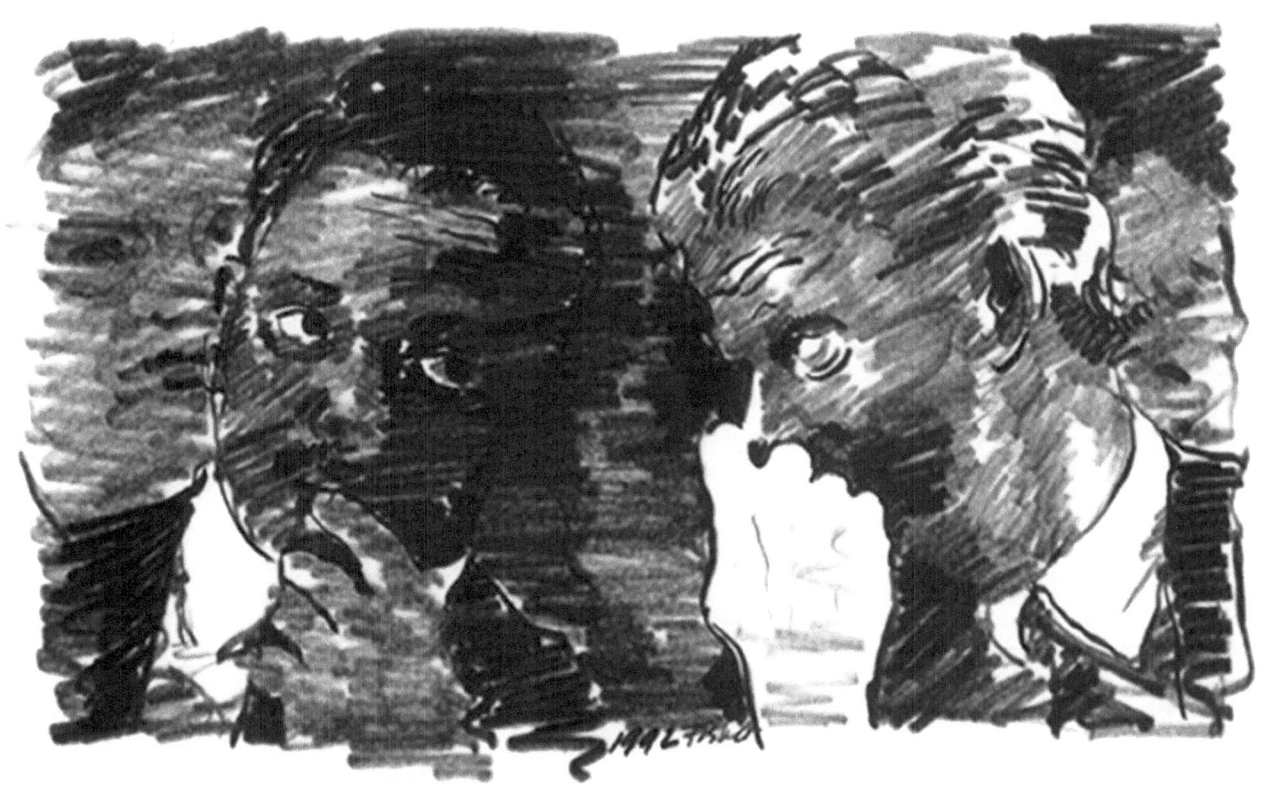

Clinton & Jackson
Graphite on Mylar Film

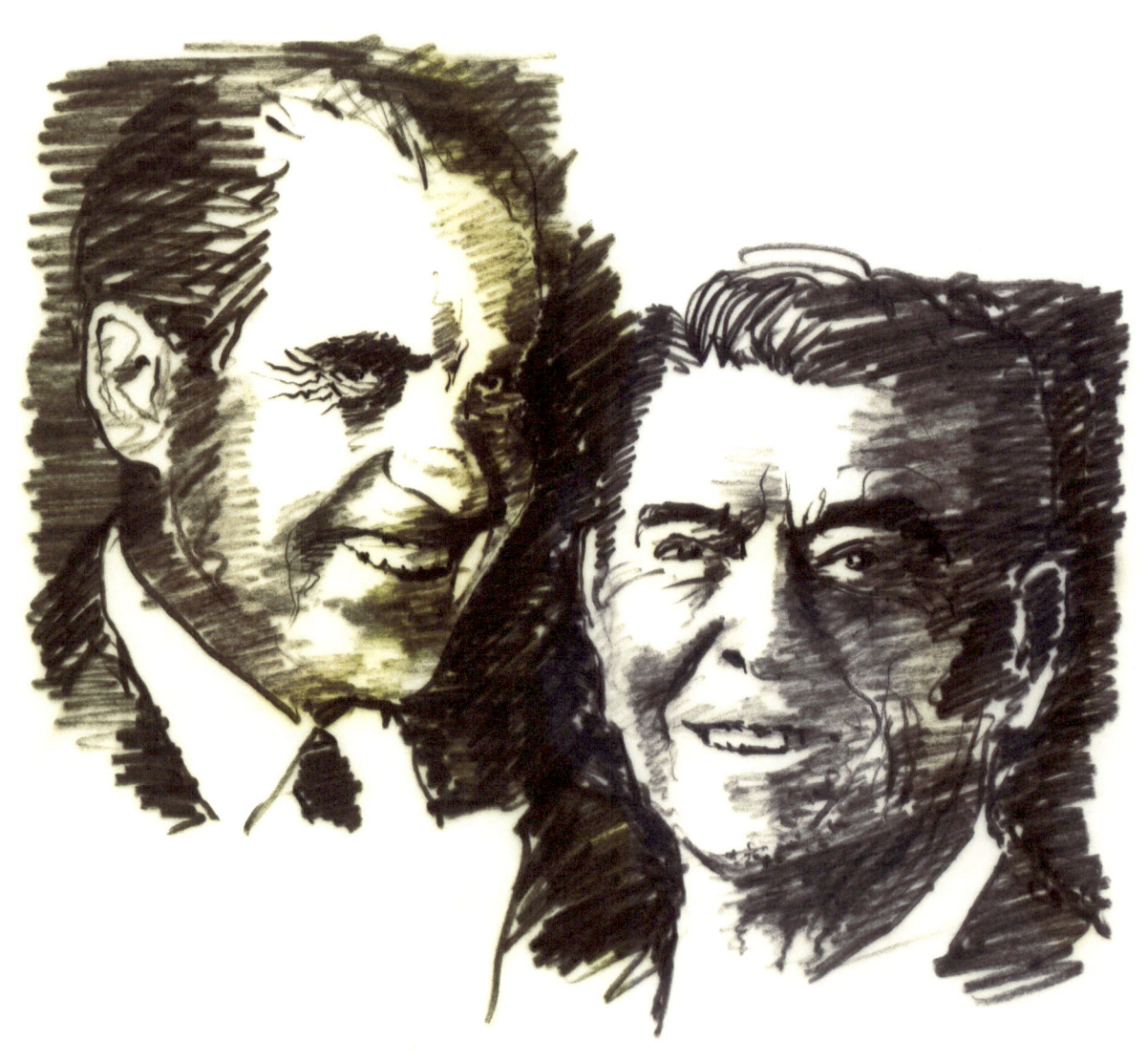

Nixon and Reagan
Graphite on Mylar Film

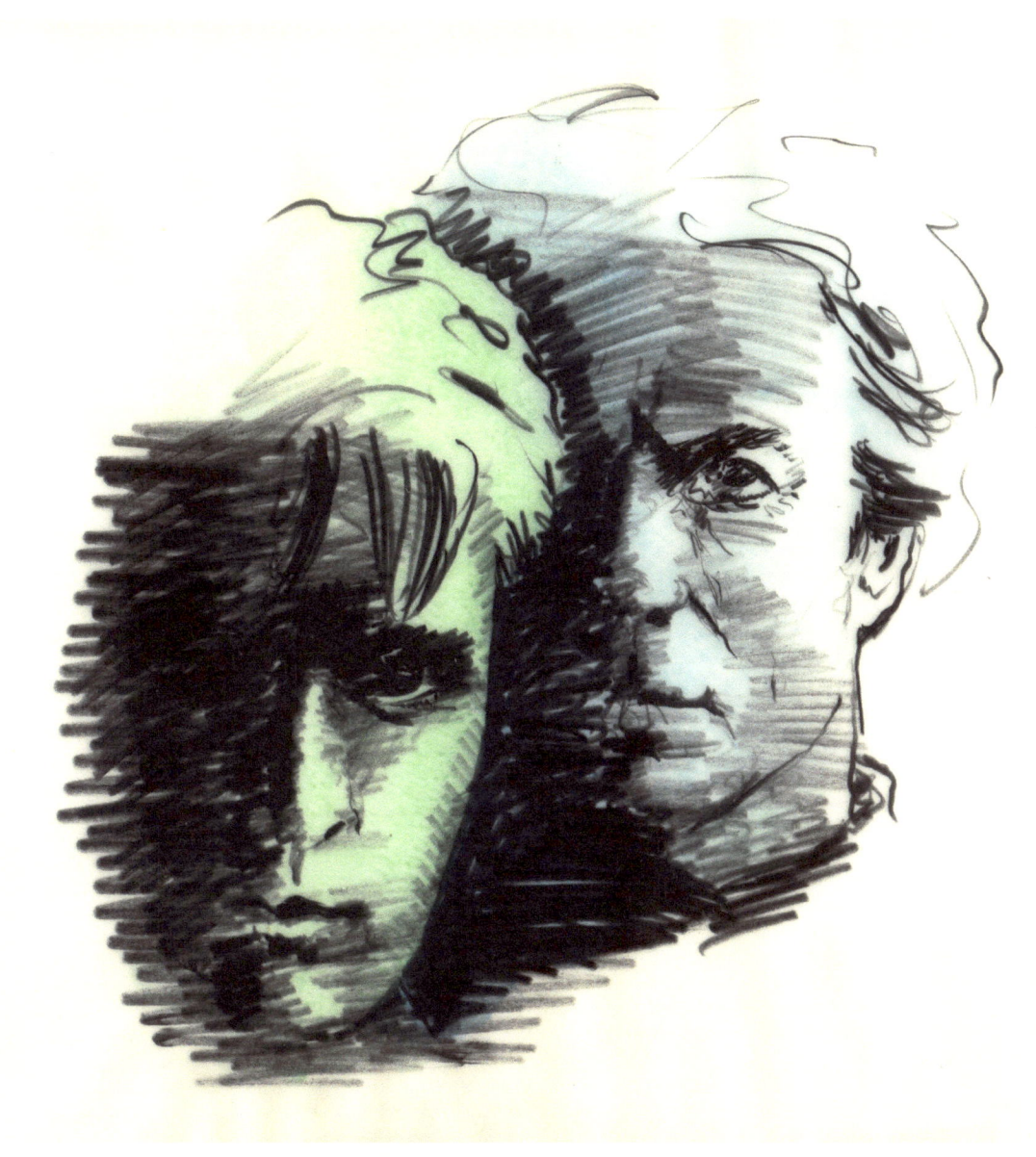

David and Yoga Pupil
Graphite on Paper

51

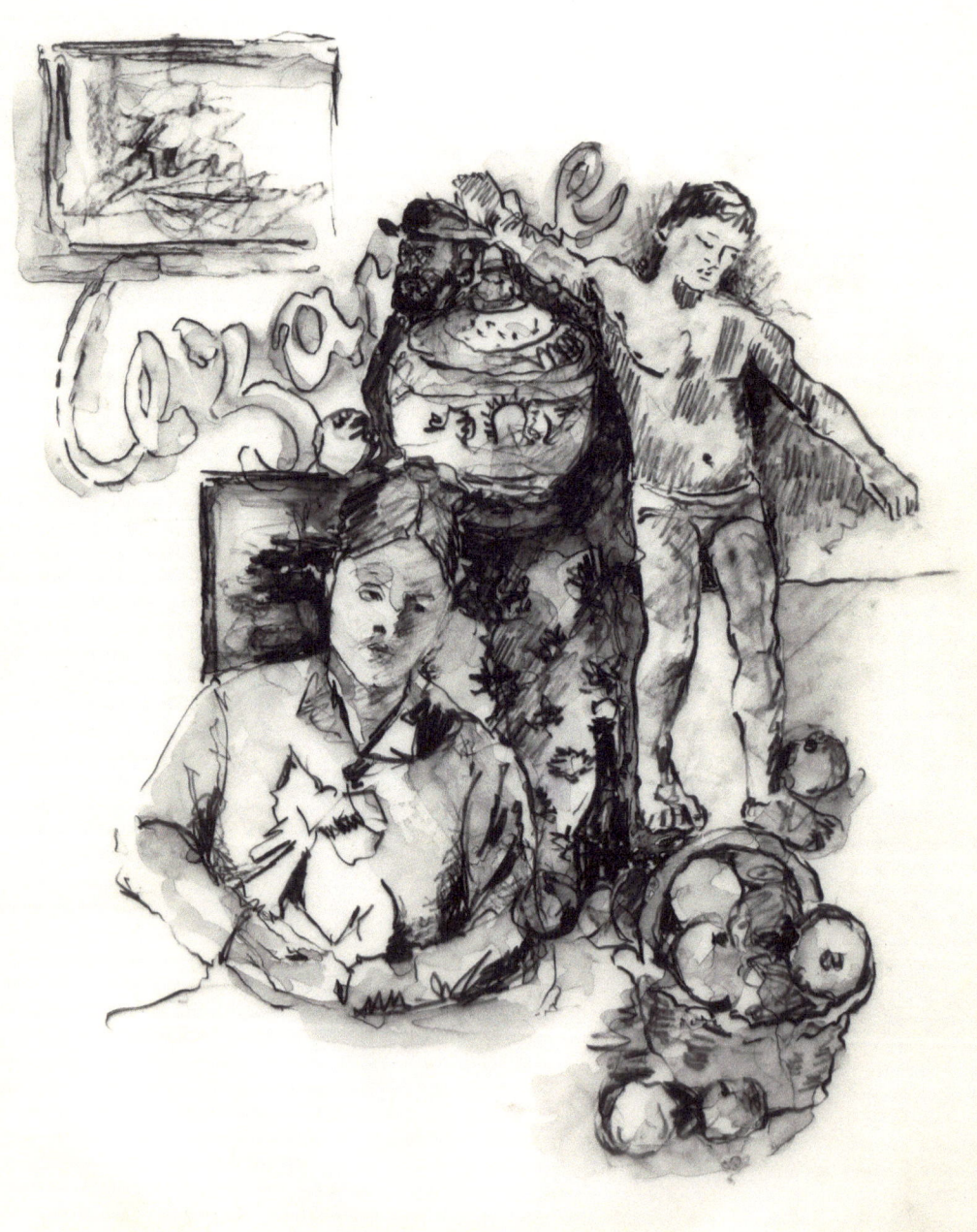

Cezanne Montage
Graphite on Paper

52

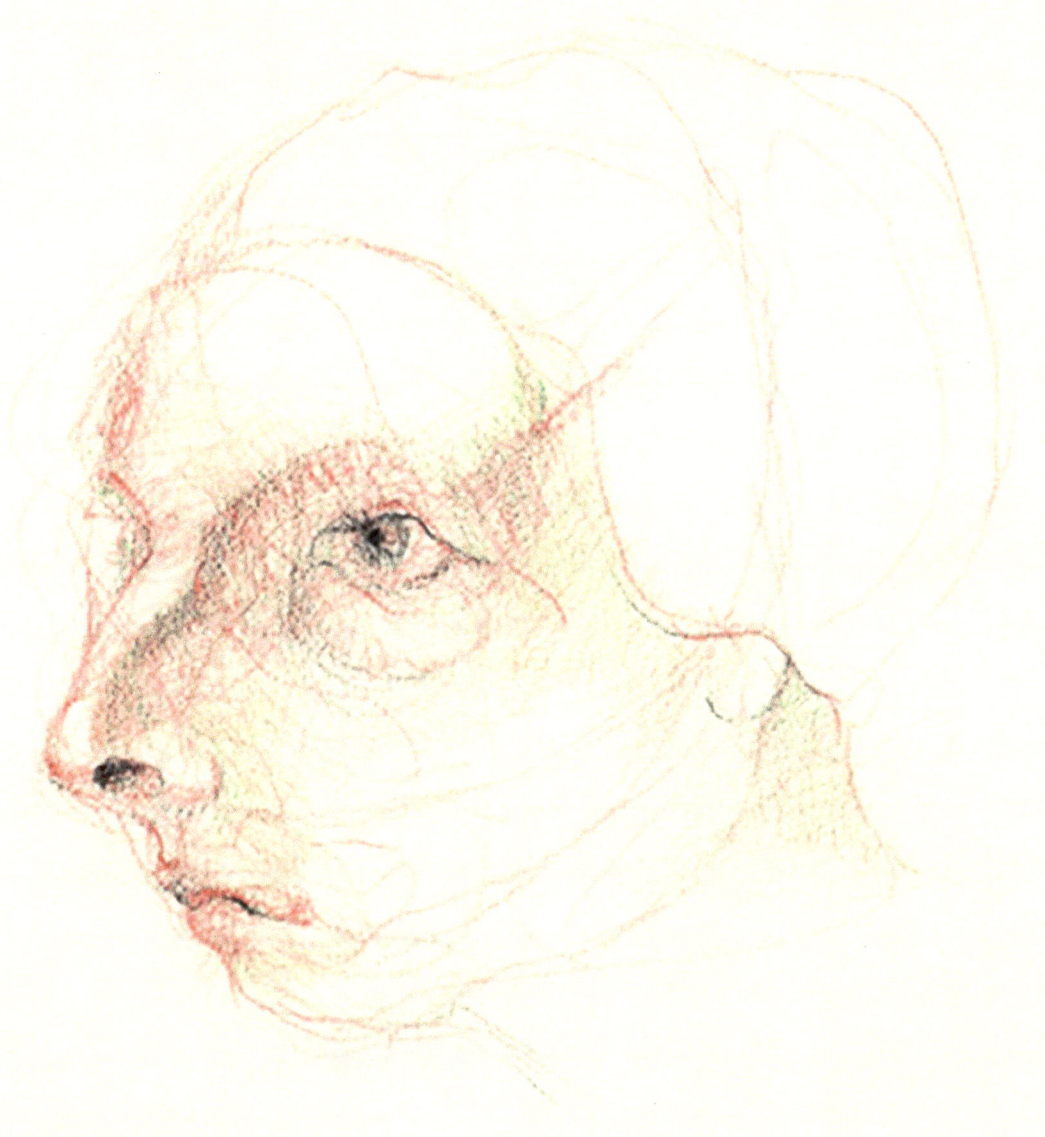

Netherlandish Woman
Colored Pencil on Paper

*Where Are You
Leonard Goldberg?*

In all relationships,
know "we are sacred
souls on a sacred
journey?

~NEALE DONALD WALSCH
Conversations with God

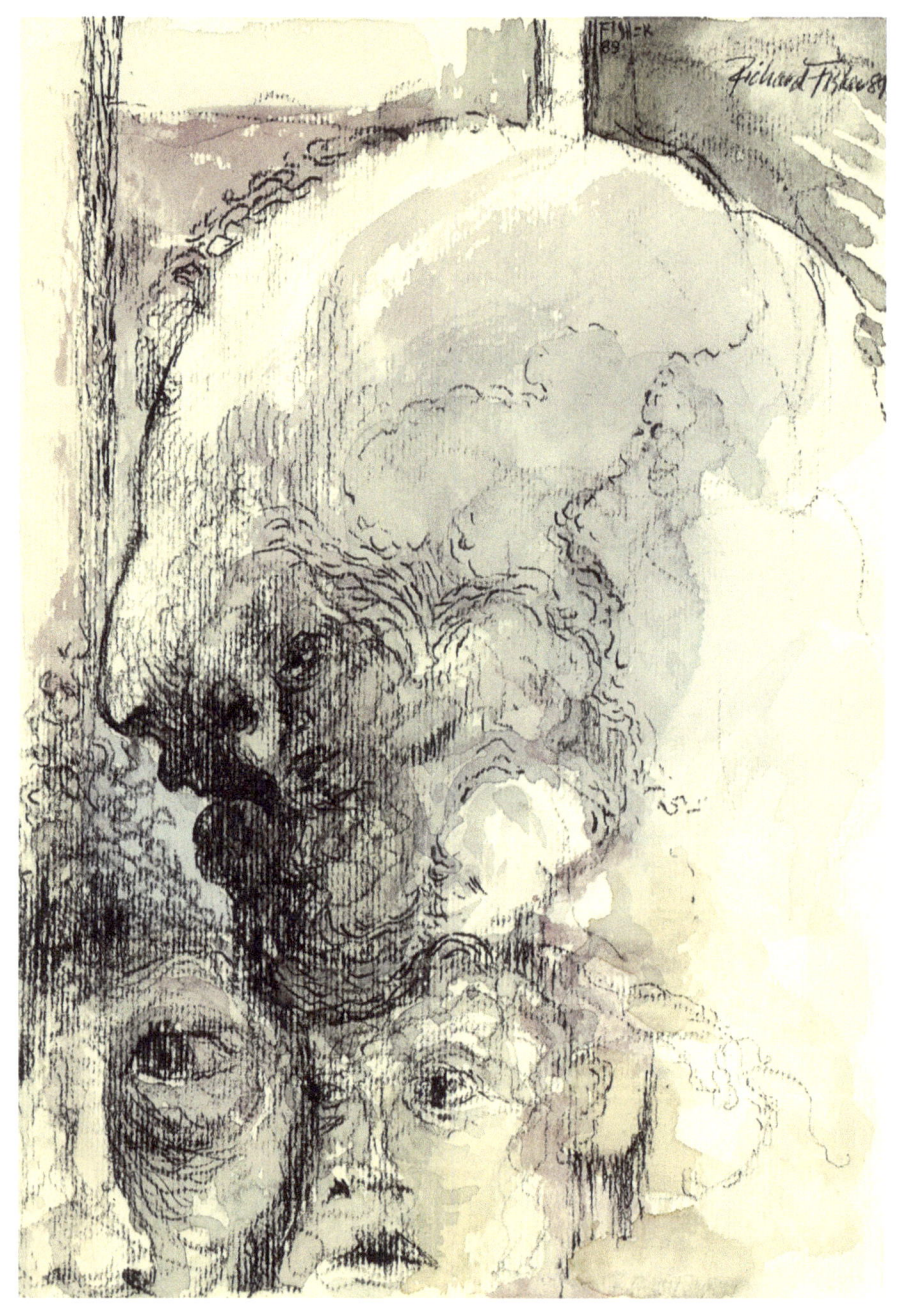

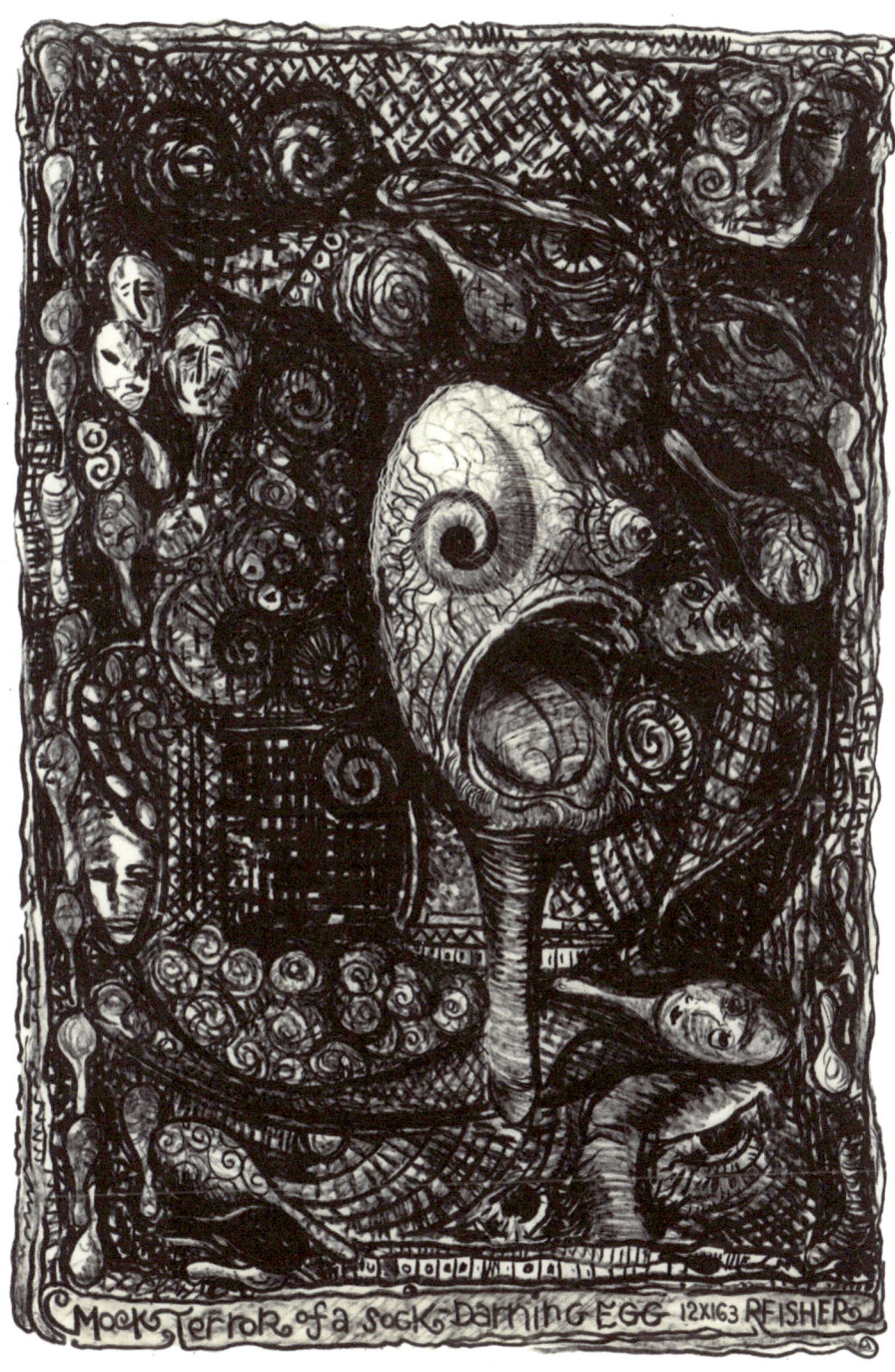

Mock Terror of a sock Darning EGG 12XI63 R FISHER

*Mock Terror of a
Sock Darning Egg*

Many years ago
people darned
their socks with a
wooden egg.

Ocean at Bridgehampton, 1963
Watercolor on Paper

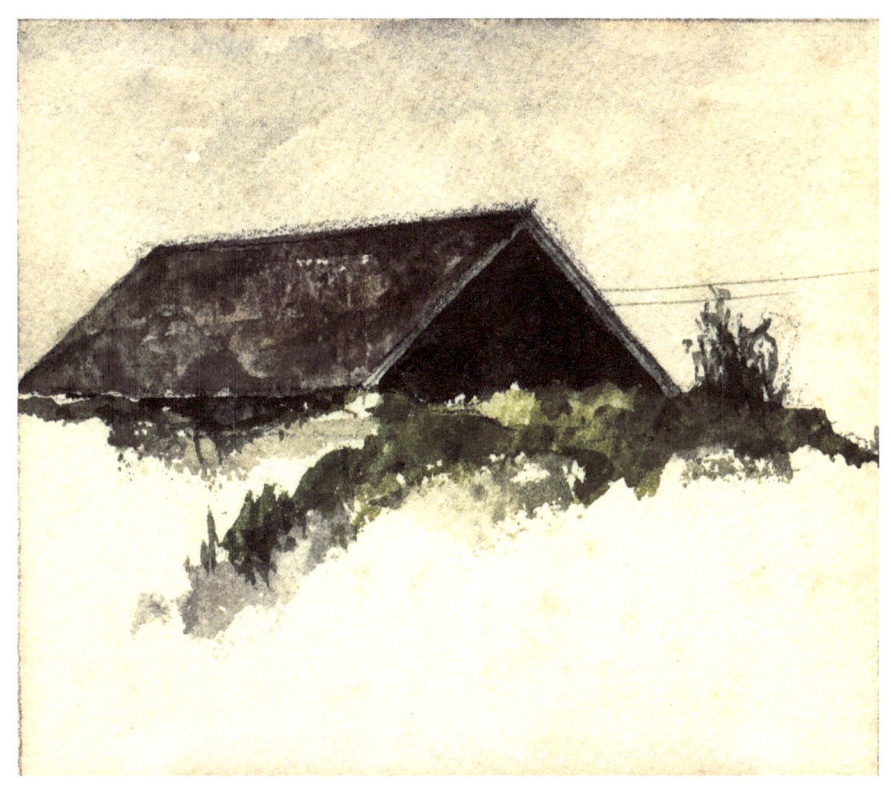

Sagaponack Rooftop
Watercolor on Paper

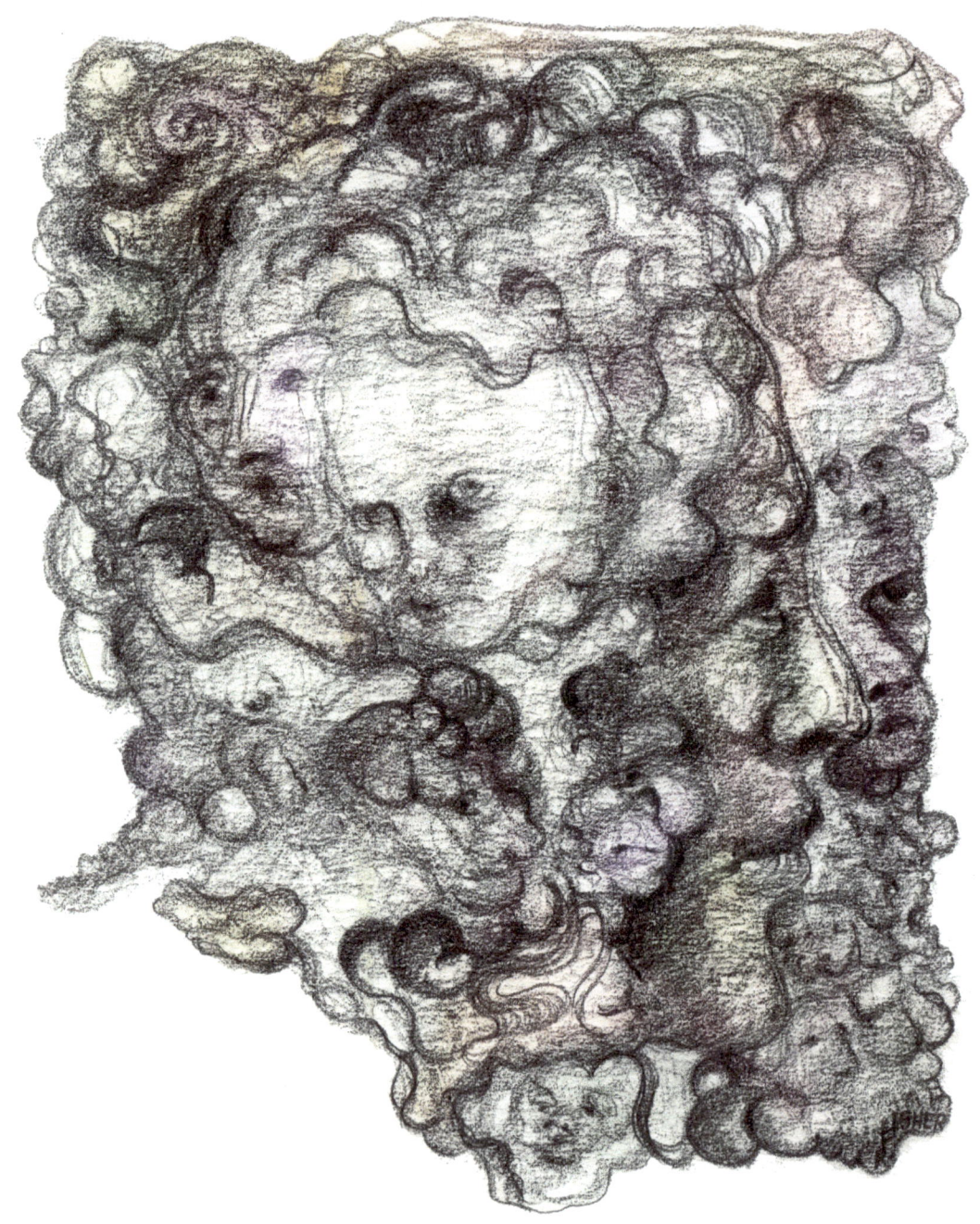

Hiding

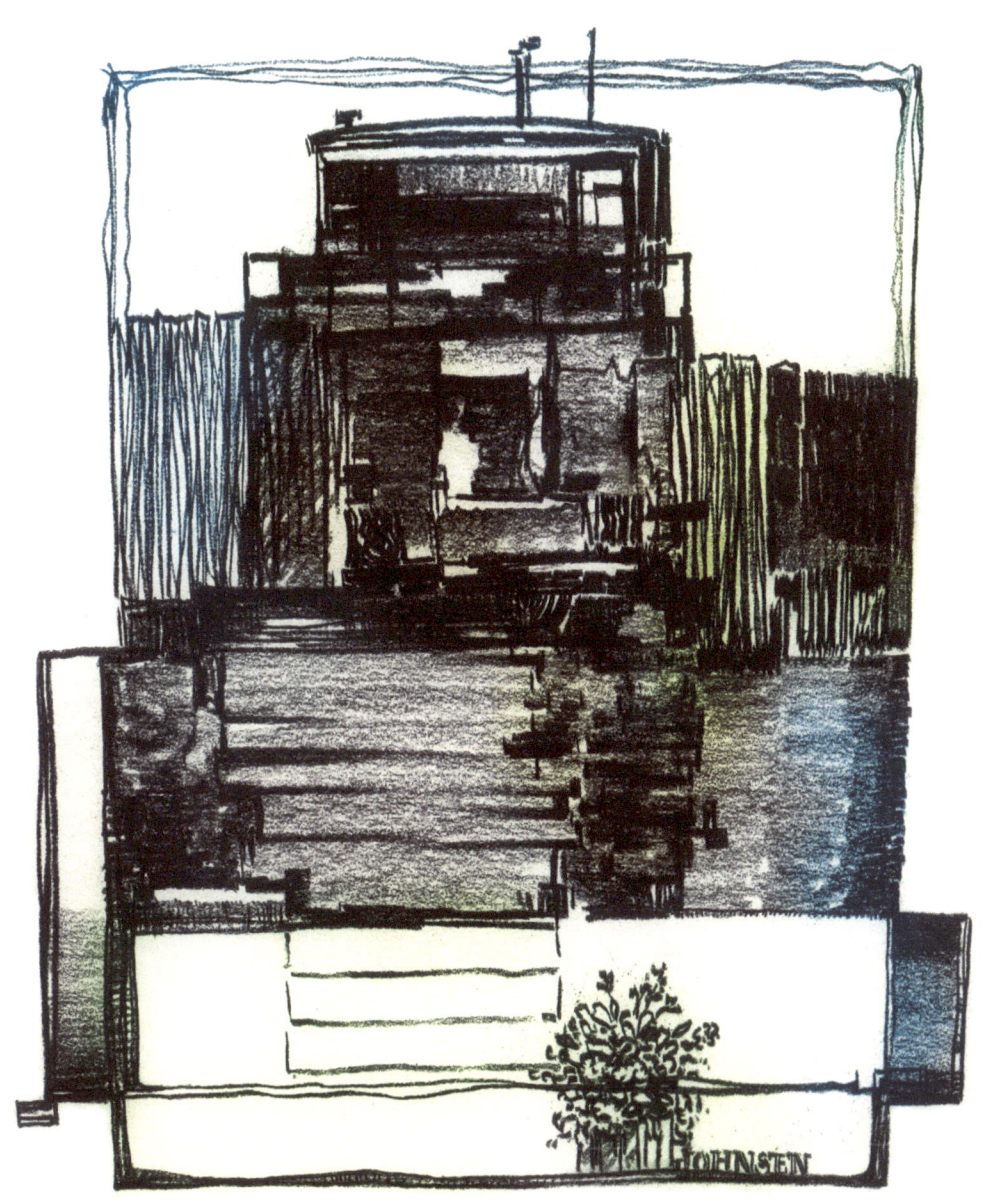

Johnsen's Barge
Graphite Pencil,
Color added in Photoshop

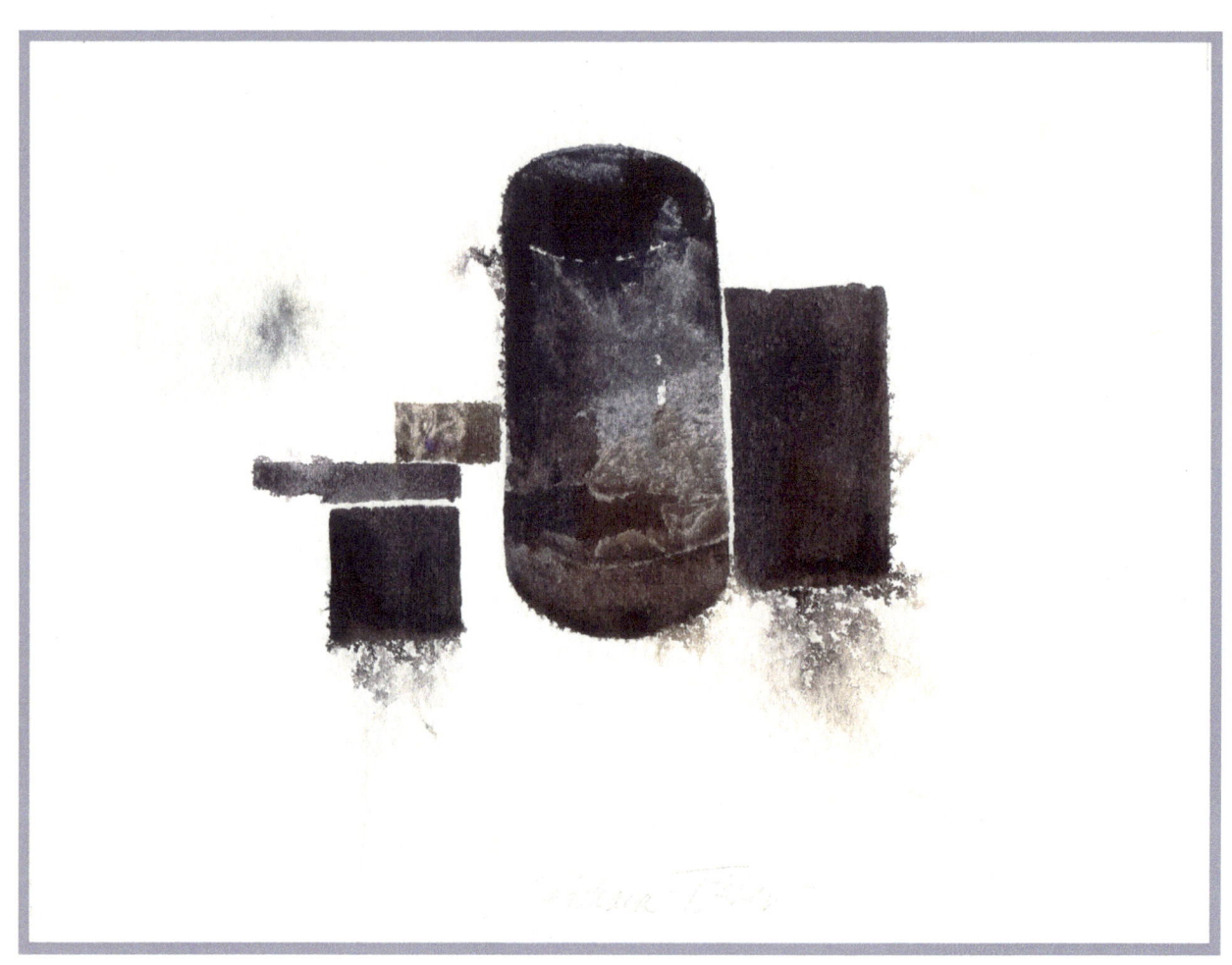

Tin with Objects
Watercolor on paper

A Brief Bio

Since the early 50's I have been continually involved with visual arts: BA degree from Pennsylvaniva State University, fine arts major; MA degree from Columbia University, Teachers' College, fine arts major; Parsons School of Design, advertising curriculum; Brooklyn Museum of Art, oil painting with Reuben Tam; extensive professonal experience in textile design, packaging design graphics, corporate identitiy programs, and finally teaching 22 years at the Fashion Institute of Technology (State Univeristy of New York) in New York City.

At FIT I taught textile (graphic) design from January 1975 to October 1997 in the Textile/Surface Design Department. Classes covered products from Home Furnishings to Apparel Fabric Prints; color fundamentals for beginning students; writing syllabi for advanced design classes in the upper division curriculum. The focus was on the current marketplace needs as well as the print technology necessary for industry. While at FIT, in collaboration with a fellow faculty member, I wrote the department textbook: *Textile Print Design*, Fairchild Publications, 1987.

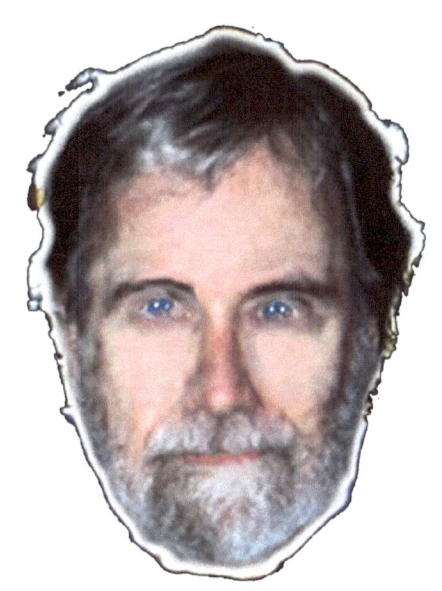

Richard

EARLY WORKS is a random selection of images, paintings and sketches, produced over a period of several decades, roughly from 1950 to 1980. Some were created during school years, others while working in industry and teaching at FIT. They are grouped into four categories: *Still Life, Figurative, Landscape and Sketchbook.* This work precedes, and in many cases, parallels the collection of MINDWORKS images, 1965-2007 also published through lulu.com

Richard Fisher